FAIR GAME

Also by Ellie Roscher

Remarkable Rose

*The Embodied Path: Telling the Story of Your Body
for Healing and Wholeness*

*12 Tiny Things: Simple Ways to Live a More
Intentional Life*

*Play Like a Girl: How a Soccer School in Kenya's Slums
Started a Revolution*

*How Coffee Saved My Life: And Other Stories
of Stumbling to Grace*

FAIR GAME

TRANS ATHLETES AND
THE FUTURE OF SPORTS

Ellie Roscher and Dr. Anna Baeth

THE
NEW
PRESS

NEW YORK
LONDON

Requests for permission to reproduce selections from this book should be made through
our website: https://thenewpress.org/contact-us.

Published in the United States by The New Press, New York, 2026
Distributed by Two Rivers Distribution

ISBN 978-1-62097-978-5 (hc)
ISBN 979-8-89385-005-5 (ebook)
CIP data is available

The New Press publishes books that promote and enrich public discussion and
understanding of the issues vital to our democracy and to a more equitable world. These
books are made possible by the enthusiasm of our readers; the support of a committed
group of donors, large and small; the collaboration of our many partners in the
independent media and the not-for-profit sector; booksellers, who often hand-sell New
Press books; librarians; and above all by our authors.

www.thenewpress.org

Composition by Bookbright Media
This book was set in Adobe Caslon and Good Pro

Printed in the United States of America

2 4 6 8 10 9 7 5 3

This book is dedicated to the trans athletes who claimed and shared their stories here, and all trans athletes, out or not, in hopes of building more fair games.

In order to protect the privacy of and promote the safety of the athletes in the book, we have changed some of the names and identifying details of the participants.

Language is alive and changes as new information becomes available. This book is being published within a particular context and the words we use here place it in time. The language will need to be updated as we learn and grow. By expanding our linguistic repertoire in tandem with our growing knowledge, we enhance our ability to communicate and to contribute to the creation of a more inclusive and just world.

CONTENTS

FOREWORD

IF YOU WERE TO ASK ME AT ANY POINT IN MY LIFE TO DESCRIBE myself in three words, the third word has varied as my interests have changed and I have matured. But *competitor* and *athlete* have been two of the three words as enduring parts of my core identity. From my earliest memories of playing organized T-ball in my backyard at age four, to being a three-sport all-conference athlete in high school, to being a Team USA athlete, sports have always been a part of my day-to-day existence.

As a young person, I knew I wasn't like the other girls in my class, but I also knew I wasn't quite like my brothers. I just always felt like "me," uniquely myself, not fitting within the confines of gender provided by my parents, my teachers, and the other adults in my life. This fact was silently understood by those around me as well. I didn't fit into the spaces made for girls. I didn't have the same interests the other girls in my class had, but I wasn't always welcomed into the spaces for boys, because as far as any of the kids could tell, I wasn't one.

Organized sports were an equalizer. They allowed me to be seen, recognized, valued, and appreciated in the same way I believed my peers were seen and appreciated off the court or the field. Sports allowed me to find common ground with my classmates and feel like I belonged.

While the topic of transgender athletes has become a political lightning rod, not everyone understands what it means to be transgender. Newspaper and magazine articles and news segments covering transgender people in sports rarely include the voices or perspectives of transgender people themselves, or of the people and organizations that support us, leading to misinformation and confusion about what it actually means to be trans.

Being transgender means that one's gender identity differs from one's sex assigned at birth. The phrasing of that is intentional: When we say "sex assigned at birth," it notes that someone else did that assignment for us. A doctor or other medical professional looks at a baby's external anatomy and assigns the baby a sex according to their visible anatomy. For most people, those designations are accurate. But for transgender people, there is a discrepancy between how we were assigned and how we know and understand ourselves and see ourselves in the world.

I did not choose to be transgender. I did, however, choose to allow people access to my truth. I view my coming out as an "inviting in"—meaning, when I publicly disclosed that

I am trans in 2010, I invited the world into my life, process, and experience.

I struggled with the idea of sharing my truth because I didn't see examples of what it might be like for me to be out in public about my identity and to continue to participate in sports. I did not see athletes who looked like me. I did not see transgender athletes participating in their sport authentically, and I did not see any transgender men competing with men, which is what I wanted to do.

When I first understood that I was transgender, I scoured the internet for examples of transgender men in sports. I didn't see anyone who looked like me. And not just in sports—I didn't see transgender men who had happy lives, successful careers, or great relationships. I had no idea what to expect or what my life might be like—I just knew that I couldn't go on living life as I was.

It was because I didn't see examples of someone like me that I decided to be out and public about my identity. Part of me wanted to move to another state, get a new job, and start over as the man I knew I was meant to be, but another part of me wanted to "be the person that I needed when I was younger," which has become my motto and guiding principle: I want to be the role model that I wish I'd had when I was a kid. I know my life would have been incredibly different had I seen people who looked like me in sports as I was growing up.

With all of the uncertainty and fear I felt about how I would be received both in and out of sports, I took solace in the idea that I could make other people's journeys more accessible, easier to navigate, and, at a very basic level, possible. Even after understanding my identity, I waited over a year before coming out because I was terrified that I would lose my ability to participate in the sports I loved.

Given the way the internet works, I knew I would only need to come out once, and then I would forever be known as "the transgender athlete." Coming out publicly was a huge relief. I hadn't realized all of the energy I was wasting policing my own behavior and hiding my truth from other people. It was like living a double life. I was constantly attentive to the way that I stood and the words that I used. I put excessive thought into how I spoke, moved, looked, and acted. I lived in fear that any one of these things might tip people off that there was more to me than they knew, and more than I was ready to share.

When I came out as a transgender athlete, there was a lot of conversation initially about "what to do with me." Sports organizations in 2010 didn't have clear policies in place to support transgender athletes. They didn't know what inclusion could look like. In every case, when I spoke with the leadership of the various sports organizations I was a part of and asked them how I could compete with the men, I was the first trans athlete in each situation to ask this question. A lot of my work as I came out was helping organizations figure out how to "accommodate" me.

This required being outed to people and organizations, explaining what transgender identity means and living through the growing pains of organizations—all at my own expense. But I knew it would be worth it.

Being able to compete authentically gave me joy I didn't know was possible. Instead of showing up to the starting lines of races and having people look at me, wondering what I was doing with the women—and wondering myself why I was at the starting line with women—I was now able to dedicate all of my time and energy into actually improving, as opposed to worrying about what other people thought of me. To be clear, it was not a narcissistic "worrying what people think of me"; it was for my own safety. Because even at that time I had a strong sense that being authentically me could put me in positions of danger.

When I came out publicly and began competing with men, I felt the world's hostility toward transgender people, but in 2010, I had no idea what would be waiting for us in the mid-2020s.

As a result of coming out publicly, I was able to seize an opportunity to create change for other people. My hope is to blaze a trail through policy and lead by example so that it will be easier for every transgender athlete who comes after me. In 2013, I launched Transathlete.com, a website that tracks trans-inclusive policies at various levels of play. I was able to use this website as leverage to create more change in sports by sharing good policies with sports organizations, which led me to consult on the creation of policies for colleges and universities, national sports governing bodies and international federations, and professional teams and leagues. Today, Transathlete.com is the leading resource for information on transgender people in sports.

Beyond creating change in policies, Transathlete.com lets

transgender athletes and their allies know that there is a place for them in sports. It gave them someone to reach out to, to know they were not alone.

Since coming out as a transgender athlete in 2010, I have met numerous athletes who have shared their stories with me. It is such an incredible gift and a privilege to be trusted with their information and to be brought in on their journey with them.

For *Fair Game*, we conducted interviews with transgender athletes ranging from ages eight to fifty-nine, from youth to professional athletes. While their stories are different from mine, with different upbringings, family dynamics, sports, and even reasons for playing, there are many through lines and commonalities. Among them is our desire to simply be athletes, without focusing on our identities. At the starting line or the first whistle, we all want to be accepted as a member of our team and to be seen first and foremost as athletes.

Sports can unify us like few other things can. Being a part of a team is a way to experience a sense of belonging. Regardless of a person's background, financial status, favorite music, or even political leanings, being a part of a team means that we work together for a common goal. Many of the athletes in this book crave not only that connection to others but to contribute and help as teammates as well.

It's easy to misunderstand people if you don't know them in real life. Lack of familiarity makes it easier to demonize people. With so much of the media villainizing trans athletes, humanizing our stories is more important than ever.

In the pages that follow, you will meet these athletes, learn about their stories, and—this part might surprise you—see yourself in their stories. I hope as you turn the final pages you will have a greater understanding of what it means to be a transgender athlete and the many ways we are all more alike than we are different.

Chris Mosier

INTRODUCTION

When we started this project in 2023, we interviewed twenty transgender people, those whose gender identity differs from their sex assigned at birth, about their experiences playing sports across a range of ages and playing levels.[1] At that time, all twenty of those athletes were able to play and compete. Our intention with the book was to share the stories of as many of those athletes as possible—to breathe life into a conversation full of people talking *about* transgender athletes without talking *to* trans athletes.

By 2026, only five of our interviewees are still legally able to participate in sports. Every athlete in our study under the age of thirty-two has been banned from participating in organized sports. The current bans that push trans athletes out of nearly all sports in all parts of the United States at every level of competition will have lasting effects on future generations.

In this book, we share the stories of these athletes, while addressing the falsehoods, myths, and fears about trans athletes that have led to their exclusion from organized sports.

Transgender people and transgender athletes have always existed, but until recently, they barely registered in public consciousness.[2] Although we have not seen an increase in the number or athleticism of trans athletes, there has been a dramatic increase in the number of people aiming to ban trans people from sports and the number of politicians vociferously barring trans people's access to public services such as education and health care as a way to garner votes.[3] In turn, folks at the highest level of organized sports are using trans athlete bans to place harsher restrictions on women athletes.

In 2024, both presidential nominees, Joe Biden and Donald Trump, commented on trans athletes in their campaigns, marking the first time high-level politicians acknowledged trans athletes.[4] Beyond visibility in political spaces, stories about trans athletes have splashed across mainstream newspapers, magazines, and sports-reporting outlets for the first time.[5] That coverage includes radicalized and politicized rhetoric that swelled into a moral panic: an outsized, morally centered response to an unrealized problem.

Banning trans athletes is a solution in search of a problem. Conservative politicians have created the "problem" of trans athletes to position themselves, along with bans, as the solution to that "problem," suggesting (if elected) they will protect women's sports, maintain fairness in sports, and prioritize women's safety in sports.[6] So, what's the problem, according to conservative policymakers and anti-trans spokespeople?

> Trans athletes are coming in droves, stealing medals, and causing harm. To protect cis girls and women, trans athletes must be stopped immediately and completely.

In response to these myths, policies to ban trans athletes have spread like wildfire. These policies are informed by a growing unease and sense of unfairness in sports, a feeling of scarcity in women's sports, and political timing and convenience. They are not, however, informed by facts. And, according to experts, neither sports nor athletes (of any identity) are benefiting from these policies.

Rather, exclusionary policies in sports have a documented history of creating climates of fear, isolation, and uncertainty. The ongoing marginalization of trans athletes isolates young athletes, including cisgender girls and cisgender boys, from experiencing healthy sports climates. The myths and the bans are *actually* doing harm.

Many people, including politicians, comment on trans athletes without knowing any personally. This is partially because there simply aren't many trans athletes. When asked their opinions on trans athletes, over 86 percent of American voters are unable to name a single trans athlete.[7] Most people rely on media coverage, or what they hear from friends, family, and colleagues, for information about trans athletes. But these sources are limited.

Trans athletes' voices, perspectives, and experiences have been ignored and silenced. For instance, of thousands of online articles written about trans women athletes by newspaper journalists, ESPN staff writers, and science bloggers, only 7.8 percent mentioned a trans athlete by name and less than 2 percent quoted a trans athlete. More articles quoted conservative lawmakers about their opinions on trans athletes than talked to trans athletes themselves.[8]

One goal of this book is to allow trans athletes' voices to counter the silence around their identities. Because in silence, shame can grow. Many of our participants talked about the pervasive default of silence around queerness and gender fluidity in their childhoods. Many had no idea they were trans because they had never heard the term or known a person who was. "It just was not talked about" was a refrain in our interviews. The silence was deafening and powerful.

We address that silence by listening to and exploring what we are hearing from trans athletes themselves. Their stories lead us to ask better questions, and those better questions invite us to challenge assumptions.

Each section of the book addresses one narrative that conservative politicians use to harm trans athletes by asking better questions and responding with data and the stories of real athletes. Beyond disproving each myth, we show how the myth does more harm than trans athletes do.

First, we interrogate whether trans athletes are "coming in

droves." Why are there so many bans restricting the participation of trans athletes when they are such a small percentage of athletes? Who are these trans athletes and what are their experiences in sports? Trans athletes are not coming in droves, and perpetuating that assumption leads to policy changes that harm all athletes.

Next, we interrogate whether being trans gives athletes a physiological and competitive advantage. Is it fair for them to compete against cisgender athletes? Trans athletes do not have a clear physiological advantage over cis athletes, and perpetuating that assumption distracts from the fact that sport is inherently unfair and that people who tend to be harmed the most by discrepancies in sport are girls of color.

Then, we explore whether trans athletes harm other athletes. Is it dangerous for trans women to compete with cis women? Are trans athletes doing harm in female spaces? Trans athletes are not causing harm, and perpetuating that assumption leads to an increase in the sanctioned policing of women's bodies and women's spaces.

Finally, we examine whether trans athletes are ruining the hard-fought spaces of girls' and women's sports. Why does gender inequity persist in sports? How can we better support girls and women in sports? Trans women are not ruining the women's category in sports, and perpetuating that assumption strengthens the scarcity mindset in women's sports instead of interrogating why there is scarcity in the first place.

A sporting culture that is safe, inclusive, and supportive of all athletes, including girls and women, is possible. Creating smart, nuanced, and relevant policies that consider an athlete's age, sport, and level of intensity while also creating pathways for trans athletes to play is possible. When we listen to trans athletes, challenge our assumptions, ask better questions, and examine the best data, we see that allowing trans athletes to compete is not a problem but a solution.

1

Who Are Trans Athletes?

Myth: *Trans Athletes Are Coming in Droves*

TRANS ATHLETES MAKE UP LESS THAN 1 PERCENT OF ALL sports participants, a statistically insignificant percentage of all athletes at the elite, college, high school, youth, and recreational levels. Trans athletes are underrepresented in all sports, at all levels of sport, in all parts of the world.[1]

Starting in 2019, the handful of trans people participating in sports came under scrutiny in the news, from politicians, and from sports organizations. Between 2019 and 2024, an egregious number of local, state, and national bills and policies to restrict or outright ban trans athletes from sports were introduced by Republican politicians. By 2025, there were thirteen times more state anti-trans sports bills proposed than there were out trans athletes.

The policymakers pushing anti-trans bans and restrictions also perpetuate the myths that justify the bans by claiming that trans athletes have an undeniable competitive advantage over cis athletes, and that they use this advantage to do harm and win. The creators of this narrative have conjured an exaggerated character who looks like a fast, strong, muscular cis man competing in girls' sports and wreaking havoc in locker rooms.[2]

This myth is fueled by fear, ignorance, and bigotry in tandem with a sense of scarcity, a sense of unfairness, and political convenience. It is effective but not informed by facts. The assumptions circulating around trans athletes, coupled with the immense number of bans proposed from 2019 to 2024 across the United States, have created a moral panic.[3]

Part of any moral panic is a disproportionate response to a social issue—in this case, the notion that there is a wave of trans athletes flooding into sports. This is simply not the case.

The Olympic and Paralympic Games—what many consider the pinnacle of global athletic competition—and the International Olympic Committee (the governing body for the Olympics) have had a policy on trans athlete participation since 2003.[4] Since its enactment and until 2021, more than 540,000 athletes competed in the Olympic Games and not a single one was trans.[5] In the 2021 Summer Olympics, two openly trans women competed: BMX alternate Chelsea Wolfe from the United States, and weight lifter Laurel Hubbard from New Zealand.[6] Hubbard's performance ended in an early exit after she failed to log a single successful lift in the first round.[7] The numbers speak for themselves: 0.0000000009 percent of

Olympic athletes in the last twenty years have been trans women, and none were anywhere near the podium.

By the summer of 2024, twenty-six states introduced anti-trans sports bills.[8] This frenzy is not driven by an explosion (or even an increase) in the number of trans athletes; participation rates for trans and nonbinary youth in sports remain staggeringly lower than those of their cis peers.[9] The number of trans athletes overall has not increased in recent history.[10]

What we're witnessing is a well-coordinated and well-funded campaign to change policies around certain groups who are aiming to access social systems, like restricting trans people from accessing sports and dismantling *Roe v. Wade* and restricting access to reproductive health care.[11] The same organizations pushing to limit abortion access are also targeting access for trans youths to health care, inclusive school policies, and sports.[12] These legislative pushes against trans kids are trickling up into higher levels of sports, leading to stricter regulations on cis women athletes at the collegiate and elite levels, such as invasive testosterone testing.

Bans against trans athletes have real impacts but are inspired by a reality that does not exist. Trans athlete participation does not reduce athletic opportunities for cis women. To the contrary, states with trans-inclusive policies tend to have higher levels of cis women participating in sport.[13] In California, where statewide trans-inclusive sports policy has allowed trans youths in sports since 2014, high school girls' sports participation in 2020 was the highest it has ever been, an increase of almost 14 percent since 2014.[14]

While the anti-trans spotlight focuses on elite sports, the real battleground is in youth sports. Less than 0.25 percent of athletes under eighteen identify as trans.[15] Yet, those athletes are forced to navigate a maze of inconsistent policies, whether at the international, national, or state level. Combined with the challenges of accessing safe medical care, appropriate facilities, and even proper equipment and clothing, participation in sports becomes even more difficult.[16] Cis athletes, who do not face such obstacles, are given a head start just by virtue of their gender.

The fictious image of a hyperathletic "biological male" trans woman athlete prevails, in part, because of the absence of trans athletes' voices, perspectives, and experiences. So, who are trans athletes? They are kids and adults who love to play. They are athletes like Eli and Dew.

Eli is a trans man who played on a boys' soccer team from age seven to twelve, even though he was being raised as a girl. He loved it. He thought of himself as one of the boys. It was logical to him, then, that he was on the boys' team. He remembers thinking of *tomboy* as its own gender, like he would grow up to be something different from a boy or a girl. "I didn't object to being seen as a girl as long as I wasn't treated like a girl. 'Girl' to me was just a biological fact of nature. It wasn't an identity."

As a trans man, Eli competes as a professional skydiver. He describes skydiving as ultimate play. When he is diving, there is no thought of emails or what he will make for dinner. He is present to the task at hand, which is staying alive while pulling off stunts in groups falling through the sky. His whole world is right in front of him, in the present moment, and his focus is optimized. He explains it as having soft eyes and a wide field of vision. He uses the word *sublime* and the phrase *perfect presence.* "It feels like your field of view is just right, your focus is just right. You're in tune with all the parts of your body that need to be doing things. Again, in that kind of mindless way. Not blank but not overthinking."

Dew is a trans boy powerlifter who lives in the South. In his state, youths must compete in the sex category that is assigned to them at birth, as well as use the bathrooms that align with the sex on their birth certificate. For Dew, that means competing in the girls' powerlifting category and using the girls' bathroom even though he doesn't want to and his sports opponents and classmates don't want him to either.

When Dew was fifteen, he signed up for a powerlifting class at school. He was using it to trick his body into the gym. He thought if there were a grade on the line, he might be more motivated to work out. Little did he know he'd end up loving it.

Immediately, Dew thrived in the sport. He loves testing the limits of his body and estimating how big of a weight increase his body can handle at each turn. He doesn't love waking up with sore muscles, but he loves the built-in discipline necessary to improve. He loves pushing his teammates and himself to keep hitting personal records and to lift more than he thought he could when the competition demands it. Dew is a trans boy who was raised as a girl.

Dew is good at powerlifting. Really good. Powerlifting

measures output on three main lifts: the squat, the bench press, and the deadlift. At age seventeen, Dew lifted 380 pounds in squat, 180 pounds in bench press, and 350 pounds in deadlift, for a total score of 920 pounds. Lifts of this kind require skill and practice. They require slow, absolute strength and a lot of training.

With that kind of weight on your shoulders or pressed over your head, there is no room for error. His mind stays busy thinking about technique and strategy so his body can do its job. While Dew is powerlifting, he doesn't think about gender. He doesn't think about classifications. Like Eli, he is totally in the moment, totally in his body, totally focused on form and the task at hand. All in all, he is a controlled storm, ready to explode. Being practiced in lifting and being strong gives Dew confidence. He has put in the time, and it has paid off.

Dew lives in a state where powerlifting is popular. Dew's high school has a team that competes within the women's power-lifting association. To compete, Dew and his teammates must comply with the University Interscholastic League rules. In the 2022/23 season, he won every competition he entered. At the final meet of the season, his biggest competitor was lifting ten pounds more than he was. Dew was nervous. By the end of the competition, just the deadlift remained. It was down to Dew and his main opponent. Back and forth, they both kept having successful lifts. Dew's last deadlift was successful. His competition lifted her bar halfway and bowed out. The lift didn't count. Dew became the state champion in his weight class.

Winning is fun, but it isn't what drives Dew. Powerlifting is a team sport. One teammate might have great technique, while another has positive self-talk. Dew and his teammates support one another in how they want to grow. On hard days, when he would prefer to stay home, Dew shows up for his team. He said, "It's not comfortable being in those tight suits for powerlifting. But it's finding comfort within the people around you. Because at the end of the day, it's different when your friend who you've trained with for hours and literally sweat and cried with for hours is spotting you, where you have the people that know you best, at least in that environment, and just sticking together."

As it has for Dew, sports can build cohesion and increase understanding across different social groups. Studies show that interpersonal relationships among cis and trans young people can engender empathy and acceptance.[17] In states with more inclusive policies for trans athletes, cis girls report healthier sports environments.[18] They participate at higher rates, have a higher likelihood of staying in sports, and say sports enhances their social life with more friends and more joy.

Denying trans kids access to sports denies this opportunity to cis athletes, too.

Powerlifting—like many sports—can transcend the gender binary. According to Dew, when training in the weight room, "there's no sections you have to go to or certain practices, we're all egalitarian here." Dew's coach has dissolved the gender binaries on the team. They are one team supporting one another regardless of the weight class or gender distinction. They are not girl powerlifters and guy powerlifters, just powerlifters. At the end of the day, it's you against the bar. Dew's powerlifting competitions, however, do have a gender component.

As a trans boy, Dew wants to compete in the boys' category. For high school sports, rules about trans athlete participation depend on the state where you live. In some states, trans athletes can compete in the category they align with if the athletic director and the state high school league support it. Dew lives in a state where the rule is that all high school competitors must compete in the category that aligns with the sex assignment that appears on their birth certificate. Dew was assigned female at birth, so he is forced to compete in the girls' category or not at all. Because he lives in a state where he must compete in the category listed on his birth certificate, it doesn't matter if his parents, coaches, teammates, or even opponents support him as a trans boy competing in the male category. The issue is contentious enough that he is forced to comply. This makes choosing to compete a hard choice for Dew. He doesn't just get to be a kid competing at a sport he enjoys. His body competing has become a political debate.

When Dew pulls up his competition results, he sees his name and results in the girls' rankings. It feels inauthentic. He likes winning, but he doesn't want to win the category that he doesn't align with. "As a competitor, it's always fun to see my name on top of everyone else's. But as an individual, it's definitely not fun."

Navigating bathrooms, locker rooms, and medal stands is charged. Dew wants to be seen as a person, not as a notion. He wants to be acknowledged for all the hard work he puts into his sport. He wants to be acknowledged as an athlete. "The reason why I want to be the best in my sport is because I'm an athlete. Just because I have the term *trans* in front of my identity doesn't make me any more or less as a person. I know how many nights I slept super sore and tired or how many times I've cried because someone was particularly whack to me. But I know who I am. I know what it took to get here. And other people's perceptions will not change that."

By the end of 2023, over five hundred anti-trans bills were introduced in forty-seven states. In 2021, 2022, and 2023, respectively, there were more anti-trans bills proposed than there were out trans youth athletes.[19] Many of these bills attempt to restrict the ability of trans youths to participate in sports and receive medical care.[20] They also increase the stigma around trans identity for youths who are already vulnerable to bullying and violence.[21] Trans youths are reporting an increase in anxiety, suicidal ideation, and self-harm.[22]

For Dew, bills that restrict trans athletes led to him competing in the girls' category in powerlifting. Dew also received an in-school suspension for using the boys' bathroom. He is expected to use the girls' bathroom.

When asked about how it feels to go into the girls' restroom, he said, "It's a lot of side-eyes, whispering amongst each other. They move around me. If I'm right next to them just passing by, they'll move out the way. Whenever I would enter or exit a stall, especially exit, they would double take. I had a few of my friends say, 'Oh, are you supposed to be here?' Just because they'd never seen me go into the restroom or they were just really surprised because I present myself as a guy because I am a guy. And I'm going into a girls' environment and space."

He has tried not drinking water and holding it all day so he doesn't have to go into the girls' bathroom, but this approach is hard on his stomach. There are three single-stall bathrooms in the school, and he tries to use those when he can. The librarians will open their bathroom for him if no adults are using it. It adds an unnecessary stressor to his school day that requires attention and vigilance he could be putting toward learning.

When Dew transitioned, [23] his parents went to the school board and, citing civil rights policy, asked that Dew be allowed to use the boys' bathroom. The school board initially complied but later backtracked. Dew says the number of adults in the building who will advocate for him are dropping.

Anti-trans bills like the bathroom bills layer with specific bills that ban or restrict trans athletes in a way that can be terrifying for trans kids and their families. But they're also terrifying because they reveal the shifting tectonic plates under sports. Fewer than a few dozen trans children across the country want to play sports in a category different from what was assigned to them at birth. The large number of restrictions and bans on those few dozen kids also impact the girls' and women's sports category at large. Policies and bans that need gender and sex policing to be enforced put more scrutiny on all bodies in the girls' and women's category. How will we make sure girls are girls and women are women? The female category might become more restrictive when it needs to keep growing. Anti-trans bills signal that sports are changing—by being subject to more scrutiny and more restrictions, not just on trans kids but on all kids and all women.

Dew lives in a state with a slew of anti-trans bills. He once had to decide if he was going to face the stress of showing up to testify at the state House of Representatives. Showing up at the capitol to defend your existence to lawmakers is a lot to ask of a kid. He went, and he was glad he did. He showed up powerfully and was heartened by others who did the same. He felt less alone. "I think those experiences really show you that you're not alone in it. And I think that's what is most important about that type of work because it's all about community and coming together. And really seeing that is a healing experience. It's a magical experience."

In the heaviness of having to be his own advocate and an advocate for all trans athletes, on top of being a student, a son, a friend, and a competitive athlete, Dew chooses joy. He allows himself to be a joyful kid. Dew is brave and clear. He is funny and artsy. He loves his two tiny dogs. He's a good friend. He wants people to get to know him as a person before they make assumptions about him being trans. Already, at seventeen, he is a role model for younger trans kids who might be watching. He encourages, "If it's a sport you love, it's a sport you love. I mean, sure, this gave me barriers and obstacles, but you just hop on over them or at least move them out the way for the next person."

Dew loves being on a team and experimenting with pushing his mind and body to its edge, and he appreciates the traits powerlifting is nurturing in him that will benefit him the rest of his life. His story complicates the anti-trans myths. He is a boy who doesn't want to be winning in the girls' category. Dew is a boy who does not want to use the girls' bathroom.

Writer and activist James Baldwin wrote, "The children are always ours, every single one of them, all over the globe; and I am beginning to suspect that whoever is incapable of recognizing this may be incapable of morality."[24] We know that trans children are struggling. If done right, sports could help them the way powerlifting helps Dew. It could also help their cis counterparts. Youth sports programs give kids the opportunity to develop physical skills and a sense of accomplishment, confidence, and self-esteem that everyone deserves to have.

We are a sporting nation, and sports as we know it are at stake, but not in the ways most people think. We are often told that trans girls have an unfair advantage over cis girls in sports and that trans people are taking over sport. This message is frightening and confusing. It is also false. But it's difficult to imagine a different way—where all kids get to play and all athletes get to compete, where locker rooms are safe for everyone and sports fields are arenas for flourishing, and where all the work that has been put into gender equity and all the vibrancy in women's sports continue and grow. Kids like Dew provide glimpses of what could be. Dew's teams are better because he is on them. And Dew benefits from being on those teams, too.

Trans youths like Dew are not legal adults, and they are navigating a physical, emotional, and psychological process of identity. There are all kinds of pain associated with being trans.

Often the angst and confusion happen in isolation, as a secret, as a creeping feeling of being different. Because of transphobia, that difference often feels dangerous. Every step of the way, trans folks need people to believe their process is real and to support them in addressing it. It takes incredible courage and perseverance to navigate their schools, sports teams, medical systems, legal systems, families, neighborhoods, and society at large. There is an opportunity here to believe them and support them in a way that will make us all better, together.

We say that youth sports are development programs. What are we developing and for whom? Who do we want our young people to become? What are they learning in sports that they can take with them in life? This moment we are in is significant. Legislation to ban and restrict the participation of trans youth athletes is up for debate. How the discussion and the voting go will affect the inclusivity and level of vigilance around gender and sex in the female category in sports. What are we teaching our kids? How we stand up for them—or fail to—in this moment will define us. The kids are watching. Our sports can develop kids toward limited, restrictive, punitive, scarcity mindsets, or we can encourage them to trust abundance, celebrate diversity, take risks, and feel joy. We can all learn from the courage Dew has, and we can allow him, and young people like him, to lead us into a more compassionate sporting culture that develops humans toward solidarity, inclusion, allyship, and interdependence.

The myth that trans athletes are coming in droves implies that the stakes are high so the participation of all trans athletes must be banned swiftly and completely. This is just not the case. In addition to trans athletes not being statistically significant in number, the stakes for competition are, most often, very low. In most cases, we can easily create policy that allows for the participation of trans athletes in a way that feels fair, safe, and inclusive for everyone.

Most trans athletes are not training for the Olympics or competing in the NCAA. The majority of trans athletes simply want to play and compete in the category that aligns with their gender identity. Adult recreational sports leagues and nonprofessional adult competition, for example, could allow athletes to play without categorizing participants by gender at all. CrossFit workouts and ultra running races don't need to be separated by gender. Ultimate frisbee and recreational adult soccer leagues don't need to specify how many women need to be on the field to create a fun, safe, and appropriately competitive environment. Adult recreational sports spaces could simply be an outlet for athletes to move their bodies, enjoy community, and push themselves to their best (or not). Nonelite sporting spaces could bring about healing, safety, and belonging for trans women and men. Instead, they often cause more harm to the trans athletes that seek them out.

Sports in the United States is unique; from youth recreation to professional leagues, the general consensus within the United States is that the government should steer clear of heavy-handed sports regulation.[25] As a result, historically, there weren't many federal or state laws directly governing sports. Eventually, about half the states would adopt new laws to regulate sports. In lieu of federal laws, we have a complex network of private governing bodies that manage sports, largely to support the professional sports industry.[26] This has created an environment where leagues and administrators have considerable control, especially when it comes to regulating athletes, and are often squarely focused on making money. So how does this play out for adult athletes in competitive and recreational sports in the United States? It depends on the sport, its culture, and its leaders.

Consider a sport that, for decades, has championed inclusivity: ultimate frisbee. Often just called ultimate, this sport has a rich history of mixed-gender play, which sets it apart from many other competitive sports. Ultimate has grown from a countercultural pastime into a globally recognized sport, complete with its own governing bodies and a strong emphasis on fair play, known as the "Spirit of the Game." Despite these progressive roots, even ultimate has had to confront the challenges of fully integrating trans and nonbinary athletes into its ranks.

In 2016, the World Flying Disc Federation updated its policy governing trans participation to align with the International Olympic Committee's guidelines, and Ultimate Canada followed suit with a more progressive policy the following year. By 2018, USA Ultimate had also revised its policies to be more inclusive, though the inclusion of nonbinary players has received mixed reactions.[27] While the sport's culture is built on inclusivity and respect, the reality is that gender equity, especially in local leagues, remains a work in progress.

Ultra running is another sport that could drop gender

categories without much drama and could, in doing so, arguably become more interesting and exciting. Similarly to powerlifting, there is no contact in ultra running, and it is the runner against themself. Feats of endurance like ultra running, historically, have transcended gender and have been an interesting equalizer. As always, money and privilege are factors when it comes to trail running and ultra running. Competitive trail runners must have access to mountains, and it is expensive to live by or get to mountains. Also, ultra running is extremely time intensive. Folks who work long hours to earn a living often do not have the time to train and compete. Fast trail runners can get corporate sponsorships to help with the expense of the sport, but many can't afford to put the time in to get noticed and land those sponsorships. Anti-trans policies in the sport of running are based on assumptions that trans women are inherently faster than cis women. Cis women do, however, have higher levels of endurance and quicker recovery from a higher proportion of type 1 muscle fibers, increased glycogen-sparing fat oxidation during endurance exercise, higher myocardial perfusion, and extracellular volume and myocardial perfusion stress. Bodies are complicated, and so is competitiveness. Su is a trans woman ultra runner who is working to remove unnecessary barriers from the sport so that more types of people can participate.

Su arrived at a trade show she had been to before with a skirt in her car. She had a brand-new feeling she had never experienced before: "I want to wear a skirt today. And everything's going to be okay." She had never felt like she belonged anywhere before, but on that day, it clicked. The anxiety fell away. She walked into the trade show wearing a skirt and felt calm, comfortable, and confident.

The moment was a long time coming.

As a child, Su had a lot of anxiety that she attributes to not feeling like she fit in her body. "I was assigned male at birth and so I was raised as a boy, but I could tell early on, I was not like the other boys, but I couldn't figure out why. I also knew I wasn't a girl, and I didn't fit in with them. And at least, when I grew up, it was you're either a boy or girl—there's nothing in between."

Su allowed herself to admit she didn't feel normal but quickly repressed her wonderings. Su was a quiet rule follower. She wasn't supposed to rock the boat. She was conditioned to be a perfectionist, to be the best at everything she did.

Except for Boy Scouts, Su stuck to herself. Because she didn't feel like she fit in either gender, she also felt like she didn't fit in society. Because she didn't have access to language around being trans, she assumed her failed attempts to grow into being a boy just meant she was weird. She was an outsider, and that was that.

"As a child growing up in an Indian household," Su remembers, "it was strict, and it was tough. But one thing I did really like about my dad was that he was open-minded, and he was levelheaded." She came out as bisexual to her parents in high school, and they were both supportive. Years later, when Su

was still presenting as male and married a man, her dad offici-
ated the ceremony. Yet anytime Su dressed in a more traditionally feminine way, her parents struggled.

Su was very thin, which did not run in her family. She had
some tests done, and at age fifteen, Su found out that she is
intersex. She has Klinefelter syndrome, which means instead
of having an X and a Y chromosome she has two X's and a Y.
Doctors gave her the option to take testosterone because hers
was low, which was one reason she was so thin, but she said
no. Being diagnosed was the first moment Su didn't feel so
alone. There were words, a term, and a syndrome that grouped
her with other people. There were other people under the same
umbrella of intersex that had sex variations. It was comforting.
There are as many intersex folks as there are redheads in the
world. She realized for all those years, she was trying to fit into
a group of boys that didn't reflect her body makeup. It was a
losing battle that she could finally put down.

As Su got older, having Klinefelter syndrome didn't fully
explain her feeling that she didn't fit in with the guys. It went
deeper than being thin. It was more complex than chromosomes. She started reading stories of other intersex people, and
some of their stories resonated.

Many folks described feeling like they didn't fit in and could
not pinpoint why. They didn't fit in with their gendered peers;
some were trans. It opened up some options for Su.

Su says she looks like a man, but she doesn't feel like one and
she doesn't consider herself to be one. She expresses gender
in a way that makes it obvious that she is not a typical guy.

Changing her pronouns helped open space for her to express her gender more fluidly.

She avoided sports, and it wasn't until about ten years after graduating from college that she got into running as a tool to deal with things in her personal life.

A running friend invited Su to enter a thirty-six-mile race with her, and Su took it on. That was her entry into ultra running. Su loved the intensity of ultra running and attributes her drive to growing up in an Indian American household with very high standards of achievement. "I'm engaged in an activity where I'm just pushing myself towards a goal that seems ridiculous."

The night before a fifty-mile race, Su got very sick. She showed up at the starting line anyway, looking haggard, but made it twenty miles before she stopped. "I wanted to see how far I could get, even though I knew I should not be running. I didn't eat anything. Anything I ate the night before did not stay with me. In terms of sports performance, I think the idea of always trying to hit that goal, no matter how far away it is, that's definitely a part of me."

Ultra running gives Su a reprieve from society. When she is running, she gets to be whoever she wants to be. She can let go and remember who she really is. She explores corners of her mind and feels incredible autonomy. Although she has a running group, she often runs alone. She likes the singularity of it.

"When I'm running, I'm able to just be me all the time. Because when I'm out running, it's just me. I'm on my own—I go as fast or as slow as I want. Usually, it's the latter. I feel however I feel, dress however I want to, and experience me without anyone giving me a stink eye, because there's nobody around."

There are moments that feel meditative and transcendent, when Su is in the middle of the forest all by herself, with no apparent trail ahead of her or behind her. She is utterly alone, and it is in those moments of solitude that she feels deeply connected. She is, in fact, not alone.

Su doesn't run to win. She doesn't even run to finish the race. "I want to go as far as I can or as long as I can. That's my goal. As I get older, it's seeing where my mind gets to and what I can overcome. Your mind can get into a lot of weird, dark spaces, and then you've got to figure out how to get through it. Eventually, I put that knowledge to use in my daily life."

A few years back, Su entered a thirty-mile trail run. She is a barefoot runner, meaning exactly what it sounds like: she runs without shoes. On this run, she cut her foot badly on the trail. There were only a few checkpoints along the way, and her first aid kit was bleak. She stopped at each checkpoint to assess the cut and then kept limping on. She took longer than she'd ever taken to finish thirty miles, but she finished. She learned a lot about herself in the struggle. "When I'm in a situation where things seem like they're way over the top or the situation seems like it's going to spiral out of control, I know to stop and just assess where I am, and know I'll get through it. That I'm able to get out of it, able to get back to safety."

Ultra running gets athletes to their edge. Sometimes the edge is physical and sometimes it is mental. What's looming in the back of your mind has time to surface. In nature by your-self, with a lot of time on your hands, the trail is a good place to work through what's there.

Once, Su was running with friends on a trail with a lot of fallen trees. They climbed over and ducked under fallen trees for miles. Wearing a wide-brimmed hat, she didn't see a tree where she thought the trail was clear. She clipped her head hard and fell. After the fall, she was going slowly, so she sent her friends on without her. They had walkie-talkies, and she assured them she'd meet them at the trailhead. She saw a split in the trail, one way leading to a lake and the other leading back to the trailhead. Her thoughts turned dark.

"I could walk down there and throw away my walkie and my phone and just sit by the lake until I died. Or I could go down the other trail. I stood there for a few minutes just asking myself, What do I do? What would my wife want me to do? My wife would want me to come home. So, I chose that path. It helped me realize that I can trust myself."

When Su got back to the trailhead, she looked at a map; there was no lake. She had imagined it.

Ultra running has helped equip Su with the ability to sit in hard moments, all the way, and trust they will pass. That they won't consume her. "The road can get rough and sometimes you don't want to live it anymore, but you can get out of it, too. I don't need to sit in that moment. I can just let the moment pass and keep going on my way."

People who thrive at distance running tend to be thin. And women tend to outperform men in ultra running. So, for Su, who was raised male and now competes as a trans woman, ultra running is a very interesting space in which to compete. Still, the competitive running community is not always as diverse and accepting as it claims to be.

When things opened back up after COVID-19, Su walked across the state of Massachusetts to raise money for trans, genderqueer, and intersex rights. She received a lot of interest and support, and it felt like the first step toward something bigger. "Can we gain a foothold in recognizing that there are nonbinary people and trans people and that these people exist, and they don't always get great treatment?"

With two friends, Su cofounded Pride on Foot, an LGBTQ advocacy organization for runners that supports folks on how they can be more inclusive, so running can feel like a safer sport for LGBTQ athletes. It gives Su so much hope. "Even though we're just talking about running groups and local races and whatnot, what can we do? How can we make it better? Let's concentrate on the northeast and just see what we can do, see if we can have some conversations and change some policies."

Some race directors have always had men's and women's categories, without questioning if that is necessary. When Su asks them their policies on trans and nonbinary runners when there are only two racing categories, they are invited to explore their assumptions. She knows race directors who have done away with gender categories since women are outperforming men, and she knows race directors who have done away with gendered dormitories for multiple-day races, saying, "Anyone can sleep anywhere. You're all adults."

Yet there are other race directors who will counter Su with "Let's just keep running to the running. Why do we have to bring politics into it?" And still others who get very political and anti-trans, and Su tires of approaching them year in and year out asking to make change.

Ultra running seems to be a sports space that could easily drop gender categories. As Su explains, "Running is one of those sports that unless you're one of the one percent elite, you are competing with yourself. The delineations we make amongst runners are sort of arbitrary. Why do you have the gendered division? A petite woman is probably better at it than a larger woman, but we don't make that distinction, even though it matters for competitive advantage."

Trans athletes like Su challenge the simplified myths that trans women are ruining the women's category in sports. Meanwhile, trans men athletes receive significantly less attention in all mainstream media than do trans women athletes, gay cis men athletes, and cis women. Annually, about seventy-five trans man or masculine athletes receive some sort of media coverage. Typically, they are young, white, and not athletically competitive. But trans men are still affected by sports and health care bills.[28] Who are trans athletes? Some are men like Logan and Layne.

Logan grew up in Georgia and was raised as a girl. He wanted to play football and baseball but was told girls don't play those sports. He hung posters of NHL, NFL, and MLB players in his room and wore his baseball cap backward whenever he could, being careful to turn it forward when his dad was around. When he looked in the mirror, there was a deep disconnect.

Logan increasingly didn't feel right in the girls' locker rooms. At first, he thought it was because he was attracted to girls. Eventually, he knew it was more. Especially as his body started changing during puberty. He was ashamed of how his body presented, and he didn't want to show it. "I would change in separate areas because I had a lot of shame wrapped around my body, and I didn't know why. And I realized, oh, because you're a dude. You don't really belong in this changing room."

The shame and confusion became consuming, and Logan attempted suicide twice in high school. Although struggling mentally and emotionally, he still performed well enough physically to earn a full tuition softball scholarship to a Division I school. All the while, deep down, Logan believed he could have played better if he could have played as his authentic self and that he would have excelled more had he not been processing all the anxiety and gender dysphoria. When he played softball, he imagined himself playing baseball. It is not that he thinks baseball is better. He has a deep respect for the sport of softball and the women who play it; he just longed to be on the field next to him, playing as a boy with the boys.

Several years into hormone treatment, Logan felt great. "It just started feeling more right and right and right and right. The past four or five years have just felt amazing. It's like all this stress and anxiety just dissipated." He boxes now, and when he boxes, he feels the connection between his mind, hands, eyes, body, and movement. It feels like dancing. Without the shame wrapped around his body, restricting him, he can move more freely. "Now, more so than ever, I'm able to be more present in my body, feel my body, experience my body."

Also raised as a girl, as a kid, Layne played like the other boys. He had one cousin who made him play Barbies, but he was always Ken. Layne was a good kid, a rule follower, leading the way for his siblings. "We were taught that family was the most important. And because we had so much love, I guess I didn't realize how damaging the church part of my upbringing was."

Layne grew up in a Pentecostal church. His maternal grandma was an evangelist, and his grandpa was an elder. They went to church Sunday, Monday, Wednesday, and some Fridays. The community was deeply influential to young Layne. "I grew up in a box where you're going to go to hell if you sin, including the kind of music you listen to and the people you could be friends with. There was certainly no space to try to figure out who you were. You're just alive in this world." He was taught that being gay was a sin. It was gross and wrong. Sex was not talked about. Terms like *genderqueer* were never spoken.

When Layne started playing basketball, he developed the characteristics that he said, "Make me *me*: confidence, competitiveness, and the intense determination to be the best."

Layne dove headfirst into basketball. His dad was his coach, and they spent hours in the gym together. His dad created rigorous workouts, and Layne loved them. He grew up on the court with his dad coaching men's basketball. He took on the mentality that he was one of the guys. He happened to play on a girls' team, but he could take on anyone. Gender wasn't a thing in his mind. He was just an athlete. All he cared about was basketball, and most of his time outside of school and church was spent with his dad. Their closeness brought a strain on his relationship with his mom. Layne said, simply, "I wasn't the daughter that she wanted."

He played all the time, and his goal in middle school was to make the varsity team his first year in high school, which he did. Like so many kids his age, Layne idolized Michael Jordan. Layne didn't just watch him; he studied Jordan play. Jordan demonstrated to Layne that you could be fire embodied. You didn't have to miss. You didn't have to ration your competitiveness. You could dominate games. Layne also studied how Jordan led. He'd score forty points while encouraging his teammates to do what they needed to do to improve as a team. Layne was perpetually the star of his team, and he worked to bring his teammates up to his level.

On the way to one of his basketball games, his dad told him he had to show up ready to play with his game face on. If he wanted to win, he was going to have to score thirty points. Layne scored twenty-eight points, and his team lost by one. "So, we're riding in the car on the way back, and my dad is just seething in the front seat. He's just angry. He's giving it to me. He goes, 'How many points did I tell you you had to score tonight?' And I go, 'Thirty.' And he goes, 'How many did you have?' And I go, 'Twenty-eight.' And he goes, 'Well, how much did you lose by?' And I go, 'One.' And he goes, 'See! See!' I'll never forget that."

Layne was talented. He had a great shot. But he says his success came from his mind. He had a mind to play basketball.

"Do you know the game? Can you see it? Do you get down when you miss? On the next play, are you dialed in? How are you preparing yourself to play? I had the mental part of basketball, and being tough against any adversity you might hit," Layne explains. And he did hit adversity, often because of his race. "I was Black, playing on a mainly all-white team. We had a super white town just down the road. They called me the N-word and a monkey in the stands. And what did I do? I gave them thirty."

Church and basketball consumed Layne's life. His parents wouldn't let him do anything social that wasn't church related. Basketball, then, taught him how to be social, how to be a teammate, how to travel, how to connect. He does not regret missing out on things like dating and parties. He really wanted nothing to do with boys in high school and couldn't figure out why. He had no one to talk to about it. He was disconnected from his body in that regard. Basketball provided him with a safe space to avoid potential intimate relationships; if he was in the gym training, he couldn't be asked out on a date.

When he was playing, he felt like he was in control. He felt like he could be fully himself. His obsession with basketball acted like a shield, a defense mechanism, without him fully realizing it. And it earned him a college scholarship.

During an elective course in Layne's first year in college, his professor invited students to sit in at an LGBT panel. Layne sat in the front row and was combative and rude to the panelist, saying, "That is wrong" and "You are going to hell." He let lines he heard from his church rip.

Sophomore year, Layne walked into French class and saw

one of the young women from the panel. His initial reaction was, "Is she cute?" He walked up to say hi, and she recognized him. "'Weren't you . . .' And I was like, 'Yeah, but that wasn't me. That was the church.' And she did end up being my first girlfriend. My first a lot."

Layne realized he liked women. This was before Google. With little knowledge of gender identity, he assumed this meant he was a lesbian. And this meant he was going to have to lie to his parents. Lying was considered a sin, and the fear of sin and hell does not die easily. The angst about living in sin affected his grades and his performance on the court.

Layne sat down with an assistant coach on the team who was a partnered lesbian and came out through tears. She listened and comforted him. "We have resources here. People you can talk to about it to help you figure out what you want to do with your family. I got you. You're fine. You're not weird." It was exactly what he needed to hear. The coach set Layne up with a therapist, knowing Layne's family and knowing he had a long road ahead of him. As Layne puts it, "To be in a religious family in the late '90s, early 2000s, that shit wasn't cute."

Layne's parents found out about him dating women and invited him home for one of his sister's basketball games. After the game, they all went to his grandma's house. She invited Layne into her prayer room, where she, Layne's mom, and Layne's aunt attempted an exorcism on him. "They were walking around me and praying, and speaking in tongues, and laying hands on me, and fucking doing it. Like, 'Satan, get out of there.' Just aggressive. For maybe forty-five minutes or an hour. And the rest of my family is downstairs in the basement watching TV. That was maybe one of the worst moments of my life."

Coming out to his family came with broken relationships. He can see now how damaging his church was. He'll never go back.

In Layne's junior year of college, he was in peak shape. The strength and conditioning had taken hold in his body, and he felt powerful. He was cut and slim. For the first time, his chest felt more toned than soft. Masculine. His team made the NCAA tournament and got the ninth seed. His first game against the eighth seed was televised on ESPN. His dad, brother, aunt, and cousin were in the stands. He played a horrible first half. Going into halftime, he had zero points, and their team was down by ten. His coach chewed him out in the locker room, and he turned it around, scoring twenty-seven points in the second half. "And as we're making our run and I'm making moves, I'm hitting threes. I'm hitting spin moves and hitting jumpers. And over in the crowd, you can just see my family cheering and being ready. And I remember one time they went to timeout. You know how they show the crowd? And it showed my aunt. It had just showed me making a shot, and then they showed my aunt. She was just screaming like crazy."

His team won in overtime. He loved to win.

Toward the end of college, Layne started to present more masculinely in his clothing. He laughs, remembering shopping in the men's section of a department store and pretending to be on the phone clarifying the size of the made-up man on the other end of the line, who he was pretending to shop for if he got weird looks from people in the store.

In 1998, Layne got drafted into the WNBA. He was sitting in his basement, on dial-up internet, continuing to refresh the web page. Then, he saw it. His name. The WNBA didn't exist when Layne was a kid, so he dreamed of being the first woman to play in the NBA. His dad told him there would be a league for women by the time he was old enough, and he was right.

Layne headed to Sacramento for training camp. He thought of himself as a combo guard. He loved to command the floor, and he loved to shoot and score. He was short, so the coaches put him at point guard. His job was to bring the ball up the court and pass it off to his teammates. He wasn't too interested in that being the extent of his role, and he didn't play well enough as point guard in the camps to impress them. Before the season started, they sent him home. Looking back, he wishes he had had an agent. He thinks his style was a little ahead of his time and that he could have thrived on a different team that let him ball handle and shoot.

Layne got invited to play in Turkey when he was twenty-one. It was a great opportunity, and he wanted to go but was dating a manipulative woman who threatened to leave him if he went. He stayed and thought his competitive basketball days were over.

When he was twenty-six, he was working at the YMCA in downtown Los Angeles. He managed an adult basketball league there, and he'd play. He was still in great shape and was scoring forty points a game. The YMCA was across from the

Sparks stadium. One night, the owners and the manager of the Sparks were playing at the YMCA, and Layne was on fire, having no idea who they were. Afterward, the general manager invited Layne to try out for the LA Sparks.

Maybe this was finally his chance to play in the WNBA. He went home, so excited to tell his girlfriend. She responded, "How is that going to work? Won't they make you travel?" It took the wind out of his sails. He lost his confidence and didn't try out.

A bit later, Layne worked for the LA Sparks in their communications department, but it wasn't quite the same. He regrets not stepping into his dream to this day.

When Layne was thirty-six, he had a job, a home, and health insurance. Held safe in that stability, he came to know he was trans and started his medical transition. Being so attuned to his body, he noticed the difference over time. After a few years on testosterone, for example, his shooting elbow felt wide, and he realized it was because his shoulders had broadened, so his shooting stance had to widen, too. He was grateful to go through the body tumult in the context of external stability. The perseverance and overcoming were internal. "How do I overcome the anxiety or fear of how I might be received? How do I overcome the insecurities that go along with this journey?"

Being older also helped him with coming out to his family. He wanted their support, but he didn't need it. He didn't go to them seeking their approval. For the most part, his family has been great. There is the occasional slip-up, using his former name or pronouns, but it is not malicious. His brother told him

that he will always be Layne's brother and that he will always
love him and accept him, but they have never had a talk about
being men together.

The most powerful Layne has ever felt was after top surgery.
After years of hating his chest, he finally felt at home. "There is
power in looking how you were supposed to."

Before he transitioned, Layne moved through the world as
a Black gay woman. "I one hundred percent know the difference between being a Black woman and a Black man. There is
a fucking difference. A big one." He constantly has to prove to
others that he does not fit stereotypes. "Black women think I'm
full of shit. Just right off the bat. They don't like me. Very rarely
are you going to see me not put together if I have to be out in
public. Because perception for people is reality. I take more care
with how I express what I'm thinking because it just matters."

Moving through the world as a Black man, his awareness is
heightened. He can feel people's alarm rise around him. One
day he saw a white woman grab her purse while he walked by.
He used to experience racism and homophobia, but he wasn't
seen as a threat. He was not treated well, but he was not feared.
Women didn't look at him and assume he was dangerous. Now,
Layne says, they do.

Six years into his transition, Layne has a complicated relationship with basketball. It is a game he loves. It paid his way
through college. He is proud of what he worked for and accom-
plished. And yet, he hesitates to go back to alumni events. He
wonders if people who knew him before are seeing him for who
he is or remembering him as he used to present. He wonders

how the cis men in his life are sizing him up. "I have great guy friends. We talk about some things, and I know how I'm viewed. But it's just like you got a missing piece."

Layne coaches, and when his players ask to see tape of when he was young, part of him wants to show them how to play hard and win. But it is hard to reconcile those memories with who he is today. When Layne is coaching basketball, he thinks back to being on the sidelines of his dad's practices, considering himself one of the players. There were no boys and girls, just ball players. That's the vibe he builds in his camps: "We're all basketball players."

He does believe brave coaches and administrators are the ones who can change the culture to be safer for all kinds of queer athletes. He is trying to be that coach. His message for trans youth is,

> In many cases for our population, our community, you have to do things even better than other people. You have to do more. But that's okay because it's going to prepare you to be greater when you get older.
>
> I want you here. I really, really do. We need you. We love you. We will fight. And we'll try to find a way. We'll try to find a way for you to do this thing that you love. And don't forget: You do therapy forever.

If he could coach the young version of himself, he'd say,

"Give yourself a break. You don't have to do everything. You don't have to be everything. Who you are exactly is enough, and it's good enough."

Conservative policymakers and anti-trans spokespeople have created a myth that trans athletes are coming in droves and will ruin sports. There would be nothing wrong with having a larger number of trans athletes competing, yet because of the staggering disproportionality between the number of bans and the number of athletes being banned, we look to the numbers to dispel the assumptions. The number of trans athletes in sports is very low, statistically insignificant. Less than 1 percent. The myth that they are coming in droves is creating a moral panic, and the number of bills attempting to restrict the participation of trans athletes reflects the ungrounded fear. The bans are in response to an image of a trans athlete who does not exist. When working to create humane policy and have humane conversations about gender equity in sports, let's let trans athletes like Eli, Dew, Su, Logan, and Layne speak for themselves.

2

Is It Unfair for Trans Athletes to Compete?

Myth: *Trans Athletes Are Stealing Medals*

THE MOST PERVASIVE ASSUMPTION, AND ONE NOT TO BE OVER-looked, is that trans women participating in sports is unfair because trans women are biologically equivalent to cis men. This narrative comes on the coattails of other assumptions, such as trans athletes masquerading or opting to transition solely to win (which has never happened in the history of sports). Or that the physiological changes that happen to men during puberty can never be mitigated, even if a man transitions to be a woman. Yet, each of these ideas focuses on fairness as a physiological "advantage" without exploring other competitive advantages that influence athletic achievements.

There are many components of this argument to break down—first, how do we know who are women and who are men? Second, what are the advantages and disadvantages women possess compared with men in sport? Third, what factors lead to someone being more athletically talented (not just taller or stronger)? Fourth, given all this information, how do we think about fairness in sport? And, finally, what decisions can/should be made based on that information?

Let's start with sex—what makes us male or female and how that affects athletic performance. It is a convenient and ubiquitous practice to categorize sex into two groups: men and women. In fact, most doctors do so through a simple visual inspection of a baby at birth and assign them a sex. Yet, scientifically, sex has never been nor will ever be considered two categories.[1] There are many biological markers of sex—chromosomes, hormones, genitalia, gonads, and secondary sex traits—and none tells us undeniably what sex someone is.[2] Human physiology is complex, and sex, according to scientists, doctors, and researchers, is better thought of as a series of spectrums, a constellation, or a mosaic.[3]

Consider chromosomes, one aspect of considering sex. Typically, a baby assigned female at birth is born with two X chromosomes, and a baby assigned male at birth is born with one X chromosome and one Y chromosome. Yet, there are XY people with ovaries who give birth, and XX people who produce sperm.[4] XX and XY is your chromosomal sex, which is different from your biological sex. There is only one gene, the SRY gene, on the Y chromosome that matters to sex. Sometimes the SRY gene transfers from the Y chromosome to the X chromosome. A Y chromosome without an SRY gene means you are physically female, chromosomally male (XY), and genetically female (no SRY). An X chromosome with an SRY gene means you are physically male, chromosomally female (XX), and genetically male (SRY). SRY deletion can lead to a person who is chromosomally male (XY) to develop a uterus and fallopian tubes, making sex categorization complex if there are only two options. SRY deletion also shows how gender fluidity is not just an identity. It is also biology.

Folks with Androgen Insensitivity Syndrome, having a body that is genetically male but anatomically female because of the testosterone receptor not functioning, often experience gender dysphoria, where one's gender and sex mismatch.[5] Medical researchers Ferdinand Boucher and Tudor Chinnah found that the brain structure of people with gender dysphoria more closely matches the gender in which they identify, pointing to a possible genetic and biological underpinning of gender dysphoria.[6]

Some babies are born with forty-seven instead of forty-six chromosomes, including XXY chromosomes, which is called Klinefelter syndrome; XYY, called Jacob's syndrome; and XXX, called Triple X. Numerous other variations include being born with forty-eight or forty-nine chromosomes. Some people have XY chromosomes but do not process testosterone like other people with XY chromosomes, which is called Complete Androgen Insensitivity Syndrome. They are typically assigned female at birth and tend to identify as female, but if they were tested, that Y chromosome would call into question which category to compete in, even though their other sex signifiers code female.

Variance goes on. Many of these chromosomal differences would go unnoticed and undetected without specific genetic testing, and many do go unnoticed among elite athletes, until certain people—usually women—are mandated to be tested.[7]

Beyond a lack of clarity about what sex is, questions often arise based not on whether people are men or women but on whether men possess other physiological features that make them more athletic than cis women (like being taller or having larger hearts and lungs).

Many scientists and exercise physiologists note that there is more diversity among men and among women in terms of athletic performance than there is between men and women. Take, for instance, testosterone levels. It is often presumed (and sometimes inaccurately promoted) that all men have much higher levels of testosterone than all women, and that "although females do produce testosterone, mainly in their ovaries, healthy post-pubertal females never produce testosterone levels as high as post-pubertal males."[8] This data is concerningly inaccurate, especially when looking at testosterone levels of elite athletes. A 2014 study by Sönksen et al. found, like nearly every study, that there is, in fact, overlap in the levels of testosterone between men and women elite athletes, with some men reporting low levels of testosterone and some women reporting high levels.[9]

Beyond the reality that testosterone levels vary between and among men and women is the fact that testosterone levels do not predict athleticism. The proxies that are often used to justify a sole focus on testosterone (for example, muscle mass, lung capacity, and bone density) are imprecise measures of athletic performance. Whether someone is male or female does not dictate their muscle mass. Height is the biggest predictor of how much muscle and muscle density someone has the potential to have. Muscle mass in cisgender men and cisgender women has the same strength when comparing equivalent cross sections by size and mass (density). Lung size is never adjusted for height, which is significant, because taller individuals have larger lungs on average, and it is also not a good predictor of sport performance. Bone density as a reason for athletic prowess is an argument that was first introduced in the 1920s to define Black athletes as subhuman and/or superhuman, and many scholars have traced this argument to its systemically racist and eugenics roots. While notions of physiology contributing to athleticism matter, how much they matter is often overemphasized to keep men and women separated.

Yet, this separation does not mitigate the reality that some athletes are just better, regardless of their sex. Take, for example, the Olympic sport of clay pigeon shooting. From 1968 to 1992, it was a mixed event open to men and women. Zhang Shan was one of six women competing in the sixty-person skeet event in the Barcelona Olympics in 1992. She shot perfectly in the first two rounds and only missed two targets in the final round to win the gold medal. She was the first and last woman to win the open competition. After the games, the International Shooting Union barred women from competing against men, and, eventually, a female category formed. Going through puberty is not an athletic advantage in competitive shooting. The timing of the sex segregation seems driven by a desire to protect men, not women.

The pervasive and oversimplified assumption that men are biologically superior to women is used mostly to separate men and women to protect the allegedly vulnerable female category of sport. Those policies have inordinately affected intersex and trans athletes but also cis men and cis women athletes.

Beyond the categorization of sports as men's or women's, to understand what is fair and what isn't, we need to differentiate between athletes who are trained in sports and those who are not.

Take Usain Bolt, widely considered the greatest sprinter of all time. Bolt's body and training made him unbeatable in 100- and 200-meter races, but when asked about running 800 meters, he stated that his best time in training was slower than that of many female athletes.[10] This isn't because Bolt is less of an athlete; it's because the physical demands of the 800-meter race are different from those of the sprints.[11] The same principle applies to trans athletes: Success is not guaranteed by gender but by how well their bodies and minds are suited to (and trained for) the specific demands of their chosen sport.

To date, only one study has looked exclusively at comparing the athletic abilities of trained trans athletes with trained cis athletes. The researchers found that trained trans athletes do not have a history of outperforming their cisgender peers at any level and, in fact, may have a disadvantage in sport, most often because of the inherent sexism and inequities that come from separating men and women athletes in the first place.[12]

These systems also serve different cultural functions that allow us to applaud some athletes but not others. For instance, there has been no comparison between Michael Phelps (a twenty-three-time gold medalist in men's Olympic swimming) and Lia Thomas (a trans woman swimmer from the University of Pennsylvania who won a lone national race).

In early 2022, Phelps publicly stated his desire for an "even playing field" in swimming, implying that Thomas had physiological advantages over her cis competitors.[13] But what's often overlooked is that Phelps himself has unique, natural physical attributes that have given him a clear edge in swimming. He has an exceptionally large wingspan and double-jointed ankles, and he produces less lactic acid than most athletes, allowing him to recover more quickly. These genetic traits are part of what made Phelps such a dominant force in the pool, but they've never been regulated or questioned.[14]

This raises a crucial point: Phelps's biological advantages are accepted as part of the sport, while similar discussions about physiological differences in trans athletes, such as with Thomas, are met with controversy and calls for regulation. The absence of any serious examination of cis athletes' natural advantages—like Phelps's extraordinary wingspan—reinforces the idea that cis men's bodies are the baseline for athletic performance. Their advantages go unquestioned, while trans women are often singled out as having unfair advantages that need to be controlled.

To create an "even playing field" in sports, we would have to consider all physiological advantages, not just those tied to gender identity.

Because men are assumed to have a physical advantage over women, gender and sex have historically been regulated in women's sport in the name of protecting the category. At first it was nude parades focusing on external sex organs, and then period tracking, and then chromosome passports. Now we are hyper-focused on testosterone. For women to prove they can compete in women's sports, some of them must prove they have an appropriately low amount of testosterone. In the conversation around fairness, then, we have to get clear on what testosterone is and what it does and does not do to our physical and competitive advantages.

Testosterone is gendered; most often, it is associated with men. Everyone—including men, women, and nonbinary people—has testosterone, and it is difficult to know how one hormone affects different people. The research is scattered and inconclusive.[15] Feminist scientist Rebecca Jordan-Young and anthropologist Katrina Karkazis describe testosterone as follows:

> This hormone doesn't drive a single path to athletic performance, nor even a small set of processes that can be linearly traced from more T [e.g., testosterone] to more ability. T is involved in many of the processes that underlie athletic performance for most people, but it should come as no surprise that it's neither a sufficient nor even necessary ingredient. . . . Just as T isn't simple, neither is athleticism separate from other human capacities: athletes must develop these capacities to a very high level, but

at lower levels, strength, flexibility, coordination, and motivation are required for basic survival. It wouldn't make any sense for us to have evolved in a way that put that range of essential capacities under the control of any singular variable, even T.[16]

Jordan-Young and Karkazis explain that different types of testosterone in different amounts affect different people's bodies at different rates and in different ways. In short, T is one factor in a milieu of hormones and performance features that make up a person.

All humans have some testosterone in their bodies, but how much changes over the course of a day and over the course of a life. The distribution of testosterone levels among elite athletes overlaps between cis men and cis women, and studies do not show a clear relationship between testosterone and performance.[17] In 2016, professors Daryl Adair and Peter Sönksen described in an article for *The Conversation*, an independent nonprofit news source, that in a study measuring the hormone profiles, including T, of 693 elite athletes across fifteen sports categories,

16.5% of men had a testosterone level below 8.4 nanomole per litre (the lower limit of the normal male reference range). Some were unmeasurably low. And 13.7% of the elite female athletes had a level higher than 2.7 nmol/l, the upper limit of the normal reference range for women. Some were in the high male range. Thus, there was a complete overlap of testosterone levels between male and female elite athletes. This challenged existing knowledge, which had assumed there was no such overlap.[18]

If regulatory bodies tested testosterone levels in female and male athletes across sports on a regular basis, they would find that higher levels of testosterone do not guarantee victory, nor do they determine whether someone ends up being an elite, Olympic-level athlete to begin with. In fact, several studies have found that higher baseline testosterone is associated with worse performance.[19] Science also disproves that the assumed advantages postpubescent men have, such as larger hearts and lungs and a lower hip-to-knee angle, lead to higher performance. All these studies are referring to adults, and nearly all are performed on cis, not trans, adults.

Even the limited research on trans athletes underscores the uncertainty around the role of testosterone in sports performance. According to the E-Alliance report from 2022, "there is little scientific understanding about the [effects of] testosterone suppression and estrogen supplementation on the physiology and athletic ability of trans women."[20] The report also notes that social factors—such as access to training, coaching, and resources—contribute to "performance advantages to a far greater extent than does testosterone."[21] Despite the lack of clear evidence, sports organizations continue to base their policies on testosterone levels, rather than on resources and access.

It's incredibly complex and the science is unsettled, which is why policies remain inconsistent, fraught, and unfolding in real time. Sports organizations must change their policies to account for such biological and athletic variability. But it's unclear how to write policy in a way that accounts for all people and exceptions. There are differences body to body and sport to sport among all athletes, even cis ones.

Trans women are consistently referred to as biological men, implying that physiologically, cis men and trans women are the same. They are not. There is a diminished physiological advantage to gender-affirming hormone treatment, and it is still unclear if any of this leads to an advantage in athletic performance. There is very little data. And it is worth noting that it seems to be acceptable to have a physical advantage as long as the body that has the physical advantage is a cis male body. Sex division perpetuates inequality instead of diminishing it.

There is little data on nonbinary and intersex folks, on trans boys and men, and on trans girls and women. Dr. Stacy Sims popularized the phrase "Women are not small men." Sims studies female physiology and how asking female athletes to train as if they are just small (read: inferior) men does not work. The same logic holds for trans athletes. We compare all bodies to cis male bodies, in large part because cis men are the ones who have been studied and tested the most. Cis men, who have historically held power and positions of influence in sports, science, and medicine, are also the ones who have asked questions, created studies, published papers, written policies, designed training programs, and come to conclusions. They have been the gatekeepers of sports and nearly all sports and adjacent research.

The placement of the line that separates men from women comes with big consequences. Human sex variance makes drawing one line to separate men and women into two neat categories impossible. But sport decision-makers are still trying.

The policies developed by World Athletics (formerly, the International Association of Athletics Federations) and the International Olympic Committee (IOC) that define who qualifies to compete as a female athlete have long been controversial. At the heart of the debate around testosterone is also the story of how policies about T were created, which starts with Caster Semenya, the South African middle-distance runner and Olympic gold medalist. After Semenya underwent invasive sex-verification testing, and in response to the media frenzy around her case, the IOC sought advice on how to better define male and female categories in sports. Experts specializing in disorders of sex development were consulted, focusing on the biology of sex rather than the science of athletic performance. This led to policies that relied on testosterone—a flawed approach. As historian Jaime Schultz explains, "An analysis of the historical and current regulations for 'femaleness' in sport, contextualized with other testosterone-related policies, reveals the impossibility of sex determination, the faulty assertion that testosterone is a 'male hormone,' and the prioritization of sporting rights over human rights."[22]

Schultz's analysis highlights a key issue: The relationship between testosterone and athletic performance is far more complex than regulatory sport policies suggest or account for. Such policies focus on medical definitions of sex, rather than on athletic performance or social context, and do not fully consider the realities of elite competition.[23] When the IOC held a closed-door meeting in 2010 to discuss these issues, they invited experts from a range of fields—scientists, sports administrators, legal experts, and even a representative from the intersex community.[24] But the working group continued to rely primarily on medical professionals in endocrinology and gynecology, ignoring the broader context of competition.

One of the fundamental questions left unaddressed by these policies is whether high natural levels of testosterone should be treated the same way we view other performance enhancers, such as altitude training or access to advanced coaching. Should athletes with naturally higher testosterone levels be required to undergo medical treatments just to compete? And what impact might these rules have on female athletes who don't conform to traditional gender norms, particularly those with naturally high testosterone or who are trans?

Beyond the science, Schultz argues that these regulations prioritize "sporting rights" over "human rights," forcing athletes to alter their bodies to fit rigid categories. While organizations claim their policies are designed to ensure fairness, they fail to consider how these rules reinforce gender stereotypes. Female athletes, particularly those who do not meet traditionally feminine aesthetic standards, are pressured to conform to a narrow idea of what it means to be a woman.

The debate over testosterone is not just about fairness. It is about identity, dignity, and the human rights of athletes. The focus on testosterone in policies, while medically convenient, raises larger ethical questions about the treatment of athletes.

Is it fair to ask athletes to change their bodies—often to harm them and their athletic abilities via hormones—simply to fit into a category that might not even reflect scientific reality? When sports organizations rely on overly simplistic understandings of sex and performance to shape sport policy, creating a sporting world that excludes, rather than includes—it's not just athletes who lose.

Let's not forget that sports themselves are incredibly diverse. A body that excels in one sport might struggle in another. There's no denying that sports require physical ability and specific skills. However, to talk about fairness, we must discuss complexity—the complexity of sex, of bodies, and of social factors. The social systems we rely on, including medicine, education, and sport, were created based on and for healthy, cis, heterosexual, white men's bodies.[25] Further, sport success is also tied to having time to train or having access to high-quality coaching and facilities, which requires money.

If we are going to talk about assumed physical advantage for trans athletes, we also need to look at the fact that there are, arguably, mental, emotional, physical, and psychological advantages to being cis that affect athletic performance. There is bodily ease and one less reason to be harassed. Secrets, confusion, doubt, and fear lead us to live in an exhausted, isolated, and constricting state that limits ease and flow, and we heard trans athletes speak of this exhaustion, isolation, and constriction as barriers to flow and performance over and over again. Several trans athletes in this book discuss how difficult it is to navigate the malalignment of their gender identity to the sex they were assigned at birth. Some athletes find sports to be a place they rest from that unrest and to just be a body moving and playing. Others speak to how the exhaustion of feeling different affects their ability to excel at play. In addition to the psychological weight, there is the cost, time, and physical repercussions if trans athletes decide to engage with care.

When critics of trans athletes assume there is a physical advantage to being a trans woman in sport, they do not consider the physical consequences of gender-affirming surgery and interventions.

For Ciara, a trans woman runner, it was running that slowed down her decision to medically transition. Her endocrinologist was a runner, too, and said her performance could take a 15–20 percent hit when she started hormone treatment. She got approved in April but did not start until the following November because she dreaded slowing down as a runner.

Looking back, she says the positives outweigh the costs. "Even just in the realm of sport, I would say the mental clarity that transitioning has brought to me has been a great benefit to, if not my performance, certainly my experience of participation in sports. I can commune with my teammates more honestly and less nervously than I ever could before."

Rhea, too, is a trans woman runner whose times dropped

significantly when she began gender-affirming hormone treatment. Her body was changing. The way she ran was changing. She changed her name and her gender marker and started running in the women's category. It was emotional—she said it was "just so great to finally do a big race as myself." What used to be running to escape became running to celebrate feeling free. Rhea is still adjusting to her body changing. Her race times are slower, but running slower is worth it to run as her authentic self.

When Rhea runs in smaller, local races, she checks to make sure her hormone levels place her in the women's category, saying, "I totally respect cisgender women. We all deserve a chance to succeed, right?"

Navigating the binary sports world is exhausting for athletes like Lennox, a trans athlete who competed in the female category in Division I soccer. Late in Lennox's college career, they came out to themselves as trans. Lennox speaks well to the exhaustion of navigating a fairly cis, straight sports system, and how they realized after coming out to themselves how their internal identity process added a weight to how they showed up and played that acted like a disadvantage. There is an ease to being cis that is hard to evaluate but could arguably be a competitive advantage, and it is an ease that cis folks often take for granted. Without even getting into the physical consequences of gender-affirming health care, Lennox's story muddies the assumption of a trans advantage.[26] Additionally, their story points to the harm that binary sports distinctions can have at the collegiate level, as well as at the low-stakes adult recreational league level.

When Lennox thinks back on their early days of soccer, the word that comes to mind is *pure*. "It was genderless," they said. Being raised as a girl, they played on boys' teams and co-ed teams until high school. They tagged along with their dad to adult league games and played on fields where age didn't matter. Winning and losing didn't matter. It was just playing to play.

Lennox was their dad's kid, following him around, playing sports. In many ways, Lennox challenged the gender binary system as a child but had no idea they were doing it. They had no language for it. They had no sense that they were existing in a binary. They were just a kid being a kid. All they knew was that they wanted to be exactly like their older brother. They said, "I had no idea that I wasn't a boy. I didn't think I was a boy, but I had no idea that I wasn't."

At the end of pre-K, Lennox's teacher asked their parents, "Do you think Lennox is questioning her gender?"

"What? No. Lennox is just Lennox."

This refrain, from a place of love, also shows the lack of language available at the time around gender. Having language gives visibility and provides possibilities.

Lennox went to a private, religious, all-girls school from kindergarten through twelfth grade. In pictures, Lennox has a bowl cut and wears boys' clothes. In high school, students came from the all-boys school to take classes. That is when Lennox started thinking about gender. "Oh, they are boys, and they are masculine and sporty. I am masculine and sporty, but I go to the all-girls school, but I don't really like all the things that these girls are doing, but I don't necessarily want to be like the boys because they're mean and icky." That is when Lennox started realizing they didn't fit anywhere recognizable on the gender spectrum.

Their parents were supportive, holding space for Lennox to be a kid outside the gender binary for as long as possible. Lennox was allowed to go shirtless on the beach for much longer than was socially acceptable, for example. Their parents didn't have the language to help Lennox navigate it all. *Tomboy* became a word that worked, until it didn't.

People started asking Lennox about their choice in clothing. They longed for school uniforms so everyone could be the same. Rather, a strict dress code with no uniform accentuated their differences. Lennox wore their brother's hand-me-down jeans instead of the tight, trendy ones their classmates wore. Lennox was fine with it until it kept getting pointed out from the outside. As high school went on, it took more and more energy for Lennox to figure out what to wear to feel the least uncomfortable while also getting the least attention. It was exhausting.

They wore dresses to dances but felt uncomfortable. So uncomfortable that their peers would comment on it. It wasn't bullying, per se, but acknowledgments like, "You don't fit in, and we all know it, and we all see it." Lennox was called a tomboy for years, but it was around high school that it felt more like a jab than an observation. Not fitting in was hard.

Playing soccer gave Lennox a much-needed respite. While they were running and playing, the binary fell away. It was the most confident they ever felt. "Playing soccer was the only place where my body felt accepted." They were just a person. An athlete. A human. Lennox found soccer captivating because they could just be a body exploring its limits outside of the scope of gender. Their body was performing, and it did not feel like a gendered performance. They had confidence in their body and in its ability to execute skills. All the players wore matching uniforms and did their job on the field. It was a safe place to be and play. "What can you train your body to do literally in mechanics and tactics? Can you execute?" There was no other expression about it.

They went on, "Before the game in the locker room, I was thinking about my body and my sexuality. After the game, I was thinking about my body and my sexuality. But during the game, you can't think about anything else, which was definitely a relief."

Lennox grew up in an affluent community and did not know a single queer person. Once they stopped expressing themselves freely as a kid, they fell right into expressing themselves as cis and straight. They dated boys. No one questioned it. Lennox didn't question it. Then, in their first year of college, Lennox came out and started dating girls. It felt liberating. And then almost immediately, they started thinking about gender, which felt new and scary. They did not know anyone who was trans or nonbinary, and they were playing on a women's college team. "I didn't really feel like there was any leeway there, so I didn't think about it for years. I just shoved it down. I felt like I got to express myself in clothes pretty androgynously without asking questions about my actual gender, which is a huge privilege."

It was difficult to navigate. It was scary to not know who to trust and confide in. Lennox didn't know where to go for support. They longed for triangle rainbow stickers adults used to put up in their offices to signal they may be a safe ally to approach. Lennox's sophomore year in college, their assistant coach was gay. They invited Lennox over for dinner with their partner. They were using she/her pronouns and contemplating using they/them pronouns instead. If you can't see it, you can't be it. The dinners felt like solidarity.

Having hours of playing soccer every day built Lennox's quiet confidence.

For years, Lennox assumed everyone was uncomfortable in their bodies. Everyone hated picking out outfits. Everyone hated changing in the locker room. That might be true, to a point. But for Lennox, the disconnect between the way their body felt on the field and the way it felt in the locker room finally got their attention. "My senior year of college was when I realized that I was definitely not a girl, probably nonbinary, and potentially trans." They didn't come out, however. "There were a few people on the team that were pretty outwardly racist, and xenophobic, and transphobic, and homophobic." Because of being on a women's sports team, because that team was very cis heteronormative and because Lennox still didn't know anyone who was gender nonbinary or trans, they kept their questioning and their identity to themselves.

Even acknowledging the disconnect between their being and their labels to themself inwardly improved Lennox's soccer game. Even though they weren't out publicly, they were out to themself, and that alignment brought more ease to their play.

I was the most comfortable with myself, with my sexuality, and quietly with my gender senior year. I knew who I was senior year. I didn't tell anybody, but I felt like that had an effect on how I was on the field. I felt more confident. I felt more free. I don't think it made me more confident in the locker room or anything like that. But, yeah, I think that's telling. I don't think it was a conscious shift. I think, in the moment, I wouldn't have known that, but looking back, it's pretty clear to me that I was playing the happiest, and the freest, and the best that I was in my senior year.

Since graduating, Lennox has told three former team members about their evolving gender identity, and they have been supportive. But Lennox has no plans to return to campus for their upcoming alumni weekend, which makes them sad. "The people that I know will be there from my team, who I love dearly as teammates and superficial friends do not share values, and I know that I would just be misgendered, and it would be a pretty harmful event for me to attend."

Even as they articulate healthy boundaries, there is pressure to be the one who puts themselves in harm's way to invite the community to elevate.

I had moments when I was thinking about my gender senior year, where I was like, "I could be the person to come out on a women's sports team. I wonder what that would be like, and who would need that representation to know that it's okay." Again, it sucks to say that out loud because I wish I was that person, but I was not ready to be that person,

and still, I could be the person that goes back for
Alumni Weekend and rocks everybody's world, but
I don't feel ready to be that person.

Now out of school, Lennox is clear on the role their community played in their becoming. "I didn't come out as gay
when I was in high school because I went to an all-girls school.
Didn't come out as nonbinary in college because I was playing a
woman's sport in college." Lennox wasn't the problem. The sex-
segregated system was limiting in a way that was problematic
for Lennox.

Lennox would like to see more identity conversations in the
context of sports teams. "There's just no conversation about
who people are, and why they're showing up the way they are,
and why they look the way they do, and their values, and how
that affects teams."

Knowing they played better when they were clear on their
identity, they imagine more identity conversations with entire
teams could improve morale and play. Think about Su, who
we met previously, and how when she pushes race directors to
drop the gender categories, they reply, "Can't we just keep it
to the running?" Lennox's point is interesting. We can't. And
if we talk about identity, where we can wholly show up and
not repress parts of ourselves or leave them at the door, athletic performance can improve, as Lennox says, "because that is
such a crucial part of being a successful team, is respecting your
teammates as full humans."

One might imagine that following their collegiate sports

career, navigating the strict gender binary system of sports has eased for Lennox. In fact, it has gotten worse. They joined a co-ed adult soccer league (which is different from a gender-inclusive or mixed-gender league), where there is a small field, ten players on a roster, and six playing per team. There must always be two women on the field per team. On Lennox's team, there are six men, three women, and Lennox. Lennox is misgendered as a woman, making four in that group, who sub out two and two.

It's understood as a fairness rule, and no one seems to question it.

Lennox feels a little stuck. A few people on the team know their identity, but they don't feel ready to come out to the other teammates, who they only see for a few hours a week on the field. They have considered speaking up about it, but they are intimidated by some of the older men on the team, and being misgendered as a woman also means they get to play more.

Although they are paying to be there and play, Lennox dreads Mondays, when they are misgendered all night long because of the two-women-on-the-field rule in an adult soccer league. Over seven months of taking testosterone, their teammates have heard their voice drop and have seen bodily shifts but have said nothing. Should they use their pronouns to register next year? It is a lot to consider for someone who just wants to play soccer. It all feels silly, while it also feels increasingly harmful.

As an adult, Lennox sees their ability to play soccer with boys and dress like a boy for years without consequences was a huge privilege. They got to learn what it felt like to play soccer outside of gender, totally free. Once you feel that, you can't unfeel it. The policies banning trans youths from playing sports, then, make Lennox livid: "I think that's the cruelest thing I've ever heard in my whole life. You should not and cannot question a child's body ever, in any way. No matter what bills and legislation come through that ban nonbinary and trans kids from playing sports, they're still going to be in sports, they're just not going to be safe, and people are going to die."

Lennox is advocating for trans and nonbinary youths and the kid that is still inside Lennox's body. They want to start a queer soccer league where folks can just sign up, regardless of gender. They imagine coming back to how playing soccer used to feel when they were a kid. Just a body running, passing, shooting, and scoring. They imagine walking down the street, putting up a few makeshift goals, and playing with other athletes for love of the game.

Lennox thought the two options they had in college were to not come out in order to compete or to quit competing and transition. This had more to do with their soccer team being cis heteronormative. The NCAA policy at the time was that transgender men who began gender-affirming hormone treatment had to compete in the men's category. Lennox was not receiving gender-affirming hormone treatment, so they weren't breaking any NCAA rules by competing on the women's soccer team. Lennox was, however, under supported in their journey as a queer athlete.

Although they speak to internal angst around being queer and trans in a sports system that often feels straight and cis,

Lennox hovers outside of the political debate around the fairness of trans athletes competing. This is in part because as a trans athlete, Lennox did not make any changes to their body or hormone makeup.

While trans women are forced to seek gender-affirming care and treatment before being allowed to compete with cis women, trans men are forced *not* to do so. If a trans man injects even a drop of testosterone, they are disqualified from competing with women's teams. They can move directly over to a men's counterpart team. However, that move is complicated, especially in collegiate sport. It requires a coach and administration on the men's side who is supportive of the athlete training and competing.[27] It requires a team of male athletes who are willing to accept and support the athlete. In nearly all cases, to move from a women's program to a men's program, trans men athletes need to learn new skills, new rules, and new cultural expectations.

Attaining gender-affirming treatment as a trans man creates a serious conundrum for athletes—they can medically transition and leave the women's sport they love, or they can medically transition and immediately be thrown into the fire of a men's team (if they're lucky). Testosterone can be difficult for anybody to take in and regulate. Injecting testosterone generally affects several functions of the body, such as insulin sensitivity. Most studies show that the effects most likely to influence athletic performance, such as changes in fat mass, lean body mass, and muscle strength, occur within twelve to sixteen weeks of starting testosterone, stabilize within six to twelve months, and

sometimes marginally continue over years.[28] Increasing testosterone can impact mood and emotions as well.[29] This means
that once they begin taking testosterone, trans men need at
least a year to allow their hormones to stabilize and to benefit
fully from T. During that period, competing in sports may not
be advisable, and/or competing in sports at a highly competitive level may not be possible. Medically and logically, it just
doesn't make sense for a trans man to start testosterone and
immediately compete for a men's team.

A boxer who began taking testosterone and was asked, a few
months in, how it was affecting their boxing, said, "Well, you
know what it's not doing? Making me stronger or faster. What
is it doing? Giving me acne."

Consider a NCAA policy, which allows practice players who
are men to compete with women athletes nearly every day.
Practice players who are men are cis students who can practice on an intermittent or regular basis with the institution's
women's teams. And they very often receive many of the same
benefits cis women athletes do, such as apparel and traveling
with the team. Of course, they don't compete with the team,
but it does beg the question: Why can't trans men continue to
stay on and practice with their teams and receive some of those
benefits too?

Regulations make it difficult for trans men to find a place, any
place, in sport. Trans men are also assumed to have an inherent
competitive disadvantage in sport, and in turn, are very often
tokenized as advocates or poster children for trans rights, without being acknowledged for their athletic prowess. The mes-

sage seems to be, we do not care about women in sports, so why in the world would someone care about trans men?

Most policies rarely work to safely include trans men athletes. The International Olympic Committee, for example, set guidelines in 2004 for trans athletes to compete in the category that aligns with their gender. It required surgery, disregarding trans men, who rarely opt for gonadectomy (the surgical removal of the testes or ovaries) as part of their transition. In 2015 and through modifications in 2021, the IOC has allowed trans men to compete without restriction. However, if they were taking testosterone and competing in women's sports, they would be accused of doping.[30]

In 2021, the now-defunct Premier Hockey Federation (PHF) and the National Women's Soccer League (NWSL) came out with policies allowing trans men to compete and take testosterone, with the PHF requiring therapeutic-use exemptions and the NWSL requiring that testosterone levels stay below 10 nanomole per liter.[31] This released trans men from deciding between playing their sport and beginning their medical transition.

There are few known trans athletes competing at the elite level, but the policies of sports governing bodies carry weight, set a tone, and trickle down to kids who have to navigate their own way.

It is not realistic or strategic to write sports policy based solely on testosterone levels in athletes in part because folks take testosterone for different reasons. One important distinction to make in the conversation around fairness is the difference between doping and gender-affirming health care. Competitive sports do have a history of athletes injecting hormones for athletic advantage, and this is different from athletes engaging in gender-affirming hormone treatment. Al's story helps clarify the distinction.

Al is a sixteen-year-old trans boy. He loves math, organizing his room, and reading historical fiction, and he describes himself as a total nerd. He loves to paint self-portraits with vibrant colors that are ugly on purpose. His oil painting started in the seventh grade. When his peers became self-conscious about flaws, he turned toward his flaws and accentuated them, realizing that pointing them out verbally and in his art rid them of shame. He loves his cat, Ginger, and his dog, Frenchie. But most of all, he loves to swim.

When Al was little, his parents put him in a slew of sports, including basketball, baseball, and gymnastics, for three months each to try them out. He hated them. He didn't like being on land, getting hot and sweaty. He wasn't flexible, couldn't touch his toes even as a kid. When he started swimming, he met other kids who couldn't touch their toes, and it helped him feel like he fit.

Al is a natural swimmer. He likes to breathe in water. His coach encouraged him to swim year-round, and he did. Al started competing in swimming when he was in the fourth grade.

In elementary school, Al had a sense that he was trans even before he knew there was a word for it. He told his friends that if he could be a boy, he would. He didn't like what people considered girl things, and he liked to wear his dad's baggy clothes. There is a picture of Al on his birthday holding a Teenage Mutant Ninja Turtle with a Donatello T-shirt on in front of his Barbie house.

> I kind of like where I grew up. When I heard stories from other elementaries in my hometown, a lot of people would be like, "Oh, yeah. So-and-so is gay, so-and-so is transgender." But my school was kind of small, so no one was really anything. So, when I went into a bigger middle school, that's when I first found out. I met my first trans friend, and I was like, "Wait. You can just switch?"

There was deep recognition in Al when he met other trans folks. There was a resounding, "That's what I am!" The knowing was immediate and complete. By age thirteen, when he was in the seventh grade, he identified as trans and came out to his close friends and teachers.

One day, his teacher accidentally outed him to his dad, writing in an email, "Al is such a great kid. I really enjoy having him in class."

Al spoke to the confusion, telling his dad that he was Al. He was a boy. His response was "Okay," followed by "I don't care what you are," and then he made them macaroni for lunch. When Al's mom came home from school, she had a few more questions but was ultimately supportive, too.

Seventh grade is also when he started competing on the high

school swim team, but on the girls' team because he wasn't fully out at school yet. At his first meet, he put down a fast time on the butterfly, and his coach said, "You're a butterflyer," and that was that. Even when competing against athletes five years older than him, he was winning.

Al swam on the girls' team in seventh and eighth grade. "Even in middle school when I knew I was trans," he said, "I was like, 'I know I want to be on the guys' team, but that's too much right now. I want to just stay on the girls' team right now.'"

In eighth grade, he was fully out, so Al and his parents went to talk to the girls' coach, and she said, "So, what you're saying is Al's a lesbian? We have plenty of those on the team."

They had to clear up the confusion.

At one meet during his eighth-grade year, he was still swimming on the girls' team but was out as a trans boy. He swam a great 100-meter butterfly at 1:07, his best time yet. He felt so proud. After the race, one of the other coaches pulled him aside and said, "My kid used to swim and was trans, but they stopped because of it. And I'm just proud to see you keep going."

Al remembered, "I beat my time. I even had someone acknowledge me. It was pretty cool."

Al switched over to the boys' team when he entered high school. It was nerve-racking for Al to officially sign up for the team. On the online portal, he had to type in his legal name and his preferred name. The next day at school, he got called down to the office and told to enter a conference room. In the room was the principal, vice principal, and other administrators. They told him to take a seat. He said he almost pooped himself.

"You are our first ever trans athlete at our school. Well, I'm glad you did this. It's not easy."

"Oh, well, thanks. Thank you," Al replied.

Then they asked him if he'd be willing to do an interview for television. He declined.

Being their first trans athlete, the school didn't know quite what to do with him. Instead of seeking outside help, they asked Al, the fourteen-year-old, what locker room he wanted to use and what they could do to support him.

They were unprepared, but they also rose to the occasion. The school turned a janitor's closet into a gender-inclusive locker room with a shower and lockers so that Al would have somewhere to change and feel safe. "I'm so cool now because I have a key card to get into my own personal locker room."

The boys' swim coach was immediately supportive, saying, "I'll take care of it, you should join the team. We want you. If anything happens, I'll actually be there."

It was an intense transition, in part because the boys' 100-meter butterfly times were significantly faster than the girls' times. Almost ten seconds faster. When he joined the boys' team, Al was more nervous than his teammates were. The first two days of captain's practice, Al didn't get in the pool. He was in a swimsuit that most people associate with girls, and he was scared.

Sports can help all kids stay active and embodied. It can help them cope with life's challenges, building resiliency, perseverance, and a sense of camaraderie. It is a powerful tool for fighting depression, building community, and cultivating lasting self-confidence. Trans young people—like all young people—deserve access to the support, care, and sense of belonging that are fostered in sport. Yet trans youths report significantly lower rates of sport participation compared with their cis peers. Although 81.7 percent of trans youths would like to exercise more, they commonly report feeling hindered by fear of exercising in public or by logistical constraints, such as financial limitations. Additional barriers include misinformed physical education teachers, social constraints around being out, anxieties around the use of locker rooms, and processes such as registering for sports.

Sitting on the side of the pool, Al was at a crossroads. The pool was an arena to practice life. Was he going to stay on the sidelines or jump in? Once he stripped down to his swimsuit, there was no way to hide his transness. There is a huge discrepancy between how people see you away from the pool and how you have to show up on the pool deck. A lot of people feel self-conscious in swimwear, and it can be even more intense for trans bodies. Al remembers, "And it's kind of like just being like the odd one out type of thing, being like the ugly duckling in a pond full of swans or something."

His friend said, "If you just keep not doing it, it's going to be way worse on the first day."

He knew that when he got in the water, people would ask questions. They did, but he was delighted that they asked "Why are you here?" They asked nicely, with genuine curiosity.

Al said, "There was this one guy who still edges me on. He is now a captain, and last year, he was a junior captain. But basically, he just really sticks up for me. I joke around with everyone; they joke back with me, but if it's someone else who normally doesn't make the jokes, who makes a hard-hitting joke about it, he actually talks to them. He gets so mad about it." When we asked Al if he had any role models, he said this teammate, because he is who he is and doesn't let other people's opinions sway his actions.

Imagine being at a big swim meet with ten teams and being the only swimmer in a girl's swimsuit. There is no hiding. He has never had any serious trouble from other swimmers. In general, no one expects him to win. "But then there's sometimes where people next to me, they'll just be like, 'Huh.' They'll give a chuckle. But then if I beat them, then they're like, 'Wow.' They just say 'Wow,' and then I get a handshake at the end, so it's okay."

At times, especially when he wins, opposing coaches will say something. He thinks it's because he is taking testosterone, which some people think will give him an advantage. They treat him like he is cheating, like he is doping, even though he has to work to gain muscle. After one meet, the opposing coach was waiting for him outside the locker room.

"I know you are on testosterone," he said.

"Really? Okay."

"I am going to report you to USA Swimming. It's against the rules."

Al's coach stepped in, "It's against the rules to take steroids. He's fine."

Al said, "The thing that kind of sucks about being a trans

athlete is that I feel like everyone just sees me as a trans man, when I just want to be a man."

It is fair to ban steroid use. Making it illegal for cis athletes to take steroids to gain a competitive advantage is understandable. Transgender athletes are working with therapists and endocrinologists to receive medically administered hormones to affirm their gender. Al's gender-affirming hormone treatment does not have the same physiological effect on him that supplementing with testosterone has on a cis boy. Al is not doping. And, most importantly, we do not have good data measuring athletic advantage in trans kids.

For Al, it really comes down to that moment when he takes off his warm-up clothes and is in a swimsuit that people associate with girls. At school, he feels almost closeted because students call him Al and use he/him pronouns. As Al says, "People just think of me as a total dude and not a trans dude."

It feels nice. He has been out for a few years, and it still feels amazing when people refer to him as a guy.

Swimming on a team helped Al contend with his feelings about his body. "I mean, even before, I kind of knew, but kind of like wearing just a T-shirt. I mean, guys and girls do that. But then, only a girl would really wear a girl's swimsuit," he explains. "I love and hate my body. I love how strong I am. Not going to lie, I kind of like how I look in a swimsuit because I can look pretty strong and muscular. But at the same time, I kind of hate it because then it's like I stand out so much."

In his swimsuit, Al feels alone, like he is the only high school trans athlete. He'd love to be able to talk to other trans swimmers like himself, who may know more how it feels. He has never met another. He'd love to make it to state for himself personally, but also as a trans athlete.

Last year, it was Al's goal to break a minute in the 100-meter butterfly. At a big ten-team meet, he thought, "Today's the day I'm going to break that minute." He stepped up on the block feeling great, swam a fantastic race, and looked up at his time: 1:00. One minute on the dot. "I got it straight on the dot, which I think is awesome." And the next meet he broke his minute, racing a 0:58.

"I love the community. I love just swimming in general because I like how my body feels," Al said, when asked what he loved about swimming. He likes having to think about his whole body, and he likes how his muscles feel after a swim. "Honestly, when I swim, I fully zone out. I'm not even thinking to the point. Because if I overthink, it's not going to work. I've done it so much, it just kind of like goes as planned or something." He goes on, "I know I want to swim in college. Even if I don't want to swim as competitively as I am in high school, I know I still want to swim in college because it just makes me happy."

If Al wants to leave his state for college, there are twenty-one states that would not let him compete in swimming in the boys' category or give him access to his medication and gender-affirming health care.

When asked what needs to change to support trans athletes,

he said, "The person just wants to do their sport. They just want to be accepted, basically. I just wish sometimes that people would just see and understand that."

Studies show that having access to sports can impart social, physical, and mental health benefits.[32] This is true across all ages and stages of development, but it is especially crucial in young adulthood for athletes like Al. In the United States, nearly seven in ten children between the ages of six and twelve engage in some form of athletics.[33] Sports can help young people build critical life skills, including communication, teamwork, and leadership, while providing a community of peers to connect with and develop positive relationships with.[34] Young people who have access to sports consistently report better grades, better health, higher self-esteem, fewer risky behaviors, and a stronger belief in their abilities and competencies.[35]

But, as kids age, they leave sports.[36] This is especially true for kids in lower-income parts of the United States, for kids of color, for kids without resources, and for girls.[37] While little research has been done on trans youths specifically, we can estimate that trans athletes are not immune to the barriers to sports that other youths face.

Many adults who want to keep trans kids from playing sports do so out of a desire to protect their own children, in most cases their daughters. The instinct to protect one's kids is an understandable one. But the truth is, banning trans kids from participating in sport is not a strategic, effective, or informed decision. The evidence is clear: In states where trans kids participate in sports, more girls participate in sports too. When trans kids participate in sports, it makes Title IX stronger. Letting trans youths participate in sports is good for their physical and mental health. It is also good for cis kids. The belief that trans girls should not compete with cis girls perpetuates the misperception that trans girls are boys. It also perpetuates a stereotype that boys are physically superior and more athletic than girls. The stereotypes about trans girls hurt cis girls too. What if all parents, not just parents of girls, invested in challenging and dismantling stereotypes that limit our kids' sense of who they can be and what they are capable of? What if instead of imagining that trans and cis girls were fighting over limited resources, we put our energy into ensuring that all kids who want to play can play?

A prevailing question has been whether laws that prohibit discrimination on the basis of sex also prohibit discrimination on the basis of gender identity. For now, the answers remain state specific. For example, in Texas, athletes must compete in the same sex category they were assigned at birth.[38] So, a trans boy like Mack Beggs must compete in the female category, if there is one. If a trans boy is undergoing gender-affirming hormone treatment, such as taking testosterone to medically transition, he is seen to be doping, which is not the same, and he becomes ineligible to compete, even though he wants to compete in the male category. In Texas, rules also force people like Beggs to use the female bathroom.[39]

In Connecticut, conversely, the Connecticut Interscholastic Athletic Conference policy allows trans athletes to compete in the category that aligns with their gender identity. In Connecticut, trans girls like Andraya Yearwood and Terry Miller could run in the female category.[40] The Alliance Defending Freedom, a conservative legal firm categorized as a hate group by the Southern Poverty Law Center, took up a case against Yearwood and Miller, stating that transgender girls are biological males, and they create an unfair culture in girls' sports.[41] Notably, U.S. District Court Judge Robert Chatigny dismissed the case in Connecticut, stating that a legally binding injury to the cis girls "would depend on a trans student running in the same events and achieving substantially similar times. Such 'speculative contingencies' are insufficient to satisfy the case."[42] Still, this is the case often discussed when considering whether Title IX gets applied to include or exclude trans athletes in the female category.[43] All of the cis athletes who sued Yearwood and Miller earned college scholarships.[44] Yearwood and Miller did not. To date, there has not been a known transgender woman who has received a scholarship to compete on a women's college team.[45] The media's spotlight on Yearwood and Miller (and other trans athletes like Mack Beggs) is a huge reason why many trans kids want to stay anonymous—to protect their privacy and to keep themselves safe.

As of 2024, over half of all trans youths lived in a state where they could not access gender-affirming health care, and according to one estimate, 38 percent of trans youths were not eligible to participate in sports in their home states.[46] By our estimates, the numbers are more extreme. Twenty-five states bar trans and nonbinary youth athletes altogether, while eighteen bar trans and binary collegiate athletes from competing with a team that aligns with their gender identity.[47]

One way to better understand how many trans youth athletes there are and how they are being affected by their states' policies is to look at amicus briefs (legal briefs filed in appellate courts by a person who isn't a party to a case but who offers relevant information to a court about the impact of a decision before the court makes its ruling) filed at the state level in response to bills focused on limiting trans athlete participation in sports. For instance, the state of Michigan and the Michigan High School Athletic Association (MHSAA) have had a policy that allows trans boys to participate in boys' sports without restriction since 2012. For trans girls, the MHSAA executive director makes determinations on a case-by-case basis, considering the sex indicated on legal documents and any medical steps that have been taken. In 2021, when a ban on trans girl athletes was proposed in Michigan, the MHSAA reported it has had an average of two case-by-case requests put forward to the executive director—out of 180,000 high school athletes in the state—a year (that's 0.00001 percent of Michigan athletes).

In 2024, there were 598 anti-trans youth sports bills proposed.[48] Add on the 604 bills proposed in 2023, the 174 proposed in 2022, the 73 in 2021, and the 29 in 2020, there have been 1,304 bills proposed over five years. Even if two per state is a gross overestimation of the number of out trans youth athletes who want to compete (and in reading other amicus briefs, there is strong likelihood that is a gross overestimate), there have been thirteen times the number of anti-trans bills proposed across the United States than out trans athletes. If we narrow this further to consider trans girls in particular, looking at the number of trans girls who file state cases to participate in sports annually, we believe that the number of anti-trans sports bills proposed across the United States is likely closer to 85 times more than the number of out trans girl and women athletes.

In the conversation about transgender adult elite athletes, many people hover in agreement with the NCAA and IOC policies circa 2019, where trans men can compete in the male or female category until they begin gender-affirming hormone treatment, at which point they must compete in men's sports, and trans women need to be engaged in gender-affirming hormone treatment for one year prior to competing in the female category, and their testosterone must test below a pre-determined marker.

In 2021, the IOC championed inclusive policies for trans athletes. The committee insisted that sports organizations should uphold fairness and equality and recognized that trans athletes do not have a clear advantage. The IOC's 2021 guidelines, still in effect, emphasize that inclusivity and nondiscrimination are fundamental to athletic policies, and they call for eligibility criteria to be grounded in scientific evidence, not based on assumptions. For this reason, banning trans women from sports goes against the global standard set by the IOC—a framework widely recognized as the benchmark for diversity in sport.

That gets complicated for trans youths because puberty happens at different times for different kids, and neither the kids nor their parents or coaches want to rush their identity formation and decisions to begin gender-affirming hormone treatment. There is simply no good science yet on competitive advantage for trans youths. Because of human variance, universal policies across ages, levels, and sports do not seem possible. But one thing is clear: Any policy that regulates trans youth athletes should center the kids' mental and physical health and encourage their participation—instead of hyper-focusing on winning.

In sports, one part of gender has remained consistent: Cis male athletes have historically been depicted as the standard—neutral, universal, biological bodies to which all other athletes are compared. Society relies on sports to "toughen" boys, denying them the opportunity to explore traits traditionally associated with femininity and steering them toward traits like aggression and competitiveness—qualities seen as markers of masculinity. As sociologist Michael Messner noted, "Boys are predestined for public lives in sport," reinforcing the familiar (and ancient polarity) scripts about what it means to be a man.[49]

Media portrayals frequently suggest that cis male athletes possess inherent qualities that make them superior in sports. Take an op-ed by Chris Surprenant, a professor of ethics, strategy and public policy, in which he writes that male athletes are just bigger, faster, and stronger than female athletes and claims that men are simply "pound for pound" more athletic than women.[50] This argument sets up a binary where male athletes are naturally superior and female athletes are smaller, slower, weaker, and less capable.[51] But that binary overlooks the complexity of athleticism. When we celebrate athletes like

Michael Phelps for his larger wingspan, hyperflexible ankles, and unique physiology, his advantages are seen as part of the expected variation among elite male athletes. Even though they are often compared with cis men, trans women do not get the same latitude for variability in ability and skill. Instead, they face intense scrutiny.

Even though cisgender women are given room to explore certain masculine traits like competitiveness, conservative policy-makers and anti-trans spokespeople frame their athletic ability through femininity and vulnerability. They're seen as needing protection, particularly from trans women.

Former South Carolina Governor Nikki Haley echoed this sentiment in a 2021 statement: "When boys compete against girls, the girls almost always lose—not just the match, but also possible college scholarships and a lifetime of success."[52] The implication is clear: Cis women need to be shielded from trans women to preserve their opportunities in sports. The underlying message is that men and women are inherently different, a narrative that preserves the privileged status of cis men, while limiting the ability of cis women to challenge the system.

As a result, trans women, more than any other group, have become the focus of fierce debates around fairness in sports. Unlike cis men, who are celebrated for their strength and speed, trans women are seen as threats. They are often portrayed as hypercompetitive, a quality praised in men but condemned in trans women. This double standard plays out in headlines and opinion pieces, dehumanizing trans women athletes and stripping them of their rights, both in and out of sports. In the news, trans women's athletic potential is frequently overemphasized, often referring to trans women as "biological men." Such language—"biological," "competitive advantage," and "inferior bodies"—fosters a narrative of stigma and exclusion.[53]

Further, trans women are portrayed almost exclusively in terms of their bodies, without room for the broader conversation about who they are as people. The narrative positions trans women as having retained the structural privileges of men while supposedly "choosing" to embrace a feminine identity. Within these narratives, trans women athletes disrupt the established gender hierarchy in sports via their feminine expression and their perceived male athleticism.

In many ways, trans men and nonbinary athletes have been erased from the conversation. The media often portrays them as equivalent to cis women, assuming they're noncompetitive and not a threat to cis men. One article even noted that "nobody's up in arms saying that trans men are going to dominate men's sports. . . . Even if they get testosterone, it's not a threat to fairness."[54] This framing suggests that trans men and nonbinary athletes will never challenge the dominance of cis men, and as a result, their ability to disrupt the gender order in sports is ignored in the prevailing discourse.

Ultimately, these portrayals of athletes reflect broader societal patterns: Cis men's dominance in sports is taken for granted, while cis women, trans women, and trans men face a range of obstacles—from erasure to outright stigmatization. In the world of sex-segregated sports, these narratives work to preserve the gender status quo, affecting trans men like Jaime.

* * *

Jaime confided in one of his roommates that he wanted to legally change his name but couldn't afford it. He didn't realize how time-consuming it would be, how many steps there were, how much paperwork was required, and how there was a fee at every turn. According to the National Center for Transgender Equality, it takes several years, hundreds of hours completing paperwork, and often thousands of dollars to legally transition. A legal transition may include changing one's driver's license, passport, social security card, birth certificate, and other legal or identifying documents, and each has their own process, timeline, and associated fees. It is estimated that medically transitioning for an adult in the United States costs anywhere from several thousand dollars to upward of $100,000.[55]

Jaime's roommate reached out to former teammates, current teammates, and Jaime's family to raise funds. To celebrate his courage, his roommate threw him a surprise party. When he got home from changing his name, there was an "It's a Boy!" sign hanging in their apartment. He received a bracelet with his new name on it and a check to cover the cost of the legal name change. He said, "It was literally one of the most moving experiences of my life."

Jaime competed in Quadball as a minority gender player, which usually means women and nonbinary folks. It was a niche role he felt comfortable in. You can only have four majority gender people (men) on the field at once. After identifying as a trans man, Jaime had to step into one of those four majority spots. Engaging in gender-affirming hormone treatment can lead to larger muscles, for example, but post puberty, your growth plates are closed, and Jaime will not get taller.[56] He didn't know if he would be competitive enough on the field to earn a spot as a majority gender player and realized, "I might lose out on my role on this team because I'm transitioning." At the same time, he noted, "I know these people will care about me and think positively of me. And I think it's more important for me to be able to live my life comfortably."

Starlet, a trans woman golfer, also shared how time-consuming and expensive it is to engage in gender-affirming health care and that there are physical consequences. She created a spreadsheet to track the cost of her process. Starlet's therapy appointments were $130 each, out of pocket. She got a referral to see a great doctor who coded the care so it would not be flagged as hormone replacement. That appointment was a $20 copay and $4 for the prescription. She paid for flights for electrolysis, and it cost $2,500 to get her gender changed on her birth certificate. And then there was the cost of her time, standing in line at the DMV to change her name on her license, sitting on hold to schedule appointments, following up with doctors. It all adds up.

Cost aside, the whole process was hard on Starlet's body. She took ten plane trips to do electrolysis, and she opted for the most intense treatment. She wanted to remove her facial hair as quickly as possible so she could be ready for facial surgery. "It is two technicians doing electrolysis on your hair follicles at the same time. And your face swells up. It looks horrendous. I mean, just brutal. But when they numb your face, over a day, there's 130 injections of lidocaine. That hurts more than the electrolysis. But then it just feels like gravel rash, like you're red and swollen. So, then it's sitting in a hotel with just ice packs. Yeah. It wasn't fun."

If we believe the myths about trans athletes stealing medals, the unfairness argument could be most prevalent in a trans woman competing in a head-to-head sport that prioritizes strength. Addison is a trans woman powerlifter whose very being challenges the assumptions about trans women. She is in a sport that could easily create pathways to participation for all athletes.

Addison grew up in a rural Midwest town where sports were king. She liked T-ball. She hated football. Soccer was fine, a nice chance to be outside. More than anything, Addison found team sports intimidating. "I knew I did not fit in with the people who played sports," she said.

Addison knew she was queer from a very young age. In Cub Scouts, when she was a kindergartener, there was a boy Addison always wanted to sit next to. She always wanted to be near him. By the end of middle school, she admitted to her friends that she was attracted to some of the boys in her class. As a kid being read as a boy, it was scary to name. She didn't know many queer people, and in her town, *gay* was used as a negative term. At a young age, Addison also learned that being trans was an option, but that it was something to be gossiped about in whispers. There was one trans woman in town who was talked about in hushed tones. Eventually, Addison dated girls but started to experiment with boys in secret.

High school years were hard on Addison. She came out as gay to her mom by writing it on a sticky note, handing it to her, and then scurrying away. Her mom came to her room and said, "I've known since you were three. Wash your hands. Dinner's ready."

Addison was pleasantly surprised and a little relieved at her mom's reaction. She had prepared herself for the worst, and the worst didn't come. What is more, she felt some constriction soften from not holding in her secret. She found it soothing that her mom did not make a big deal out of it, and it helped her feel seen and known.

Addison came out to a trusted group of people the summer between her sophomore and junior years, and by fall, her whole school knew. She felt betrayed by her friends. Out of one thousand students, she was the only one who was out as gay. She used to be taunted by popular kids for being emo and goth, but after she came out, the bullying became more aggressive and violent. What used to be nervousness about going to school became acute dread and fear.

Addison played the mellophone in the marching band and became the head drum major her senior year of high school. She considered marching band a sport, playing an instrument while marching in formation in a wool suit in one-hundred-degree weather was not for the faint of heart. Marching band and drama club were two communities where she could rest, be, and feel safe. Her hypervigilance could stop. "I didn't have to be anybody other than myself."

Leaving her small Midwestern town for a state college in the northeast was a temporary refuge compared with high school. She could be more anonymous on a campus of fifteen thousand, and she was granted more space to become herself. She said, "People didn't know who I was unless I told them." Even though the college town had one main street with a Walmart, a few restaurants, and dive bars, Addison felt like she had arrived. She joined the theater program, met other artists, and found pockets of space to belong.

College allowed Addison to grow, but her small hometown remained unchanged. In her first summer home from college, she was harassed so heavily, she never went back.

College was the first time Addison met gender-diverse people and moved within queer spaces. It was after college, however, when Addison moved to a dynamic neighborhood in a bigger city, that her world exploded. She was not interested in all that became available to her, but she loved how her world instantly expanded. "You could buy meth on any corner," she remembered. "It was rough around the edges, and I loved it."

Addison lived in a tiny apartment on the top of a hill. At the bottom of the hill was a gay dive bar that Addison soon referred to as her living room. It had a tiny stage and a cigarette-burned pool table. Drag shows were held multiple nights a week, and a punk queer crowd gathered there religiously.[57] A gaggle of older folks who presented as cis and straight at work could safely be themselves as cross-dressers on the weekends. "Honestly," Addison mused, "if they were my age, they probably would be trans women, but I just think, generationally, they weren't able to get there."

The dive bar is where Addison tried drag for the first time. Trying on dresses and makeup felt rebellious. It felt good. It felt right.

In her early twenties, Addison identified as a gay man who dressed androgynously and wore makeup. Androgyny was enough. Being visibly queer was enough. Then it wasn't.

In the safety of her queer community, she was able to say, "This is only the tip of the iceberg. I don't want to be perceived as a queer person. I want to be perceived as a woman. If I could have chosen, I would have chosen to be born as a woman."

Addison had internalized that you had to hate your body to be trans. You had to feel like you were trapped in the wrong body. That never resonated with her, so she didn't explore the possibility that she was trans. It wasn't until she was in a loving community and was loving expressing her queerness that she lived into the truth that she loved her body and that body was the body of a trans woman. She realized that she didn't have to wish she were a woman. She could just be a woman because she is a woman. She can be it because she says so.

When she came out as trans to her mom, she was probing her about her childhood. Her mom knew she was queer at a young age—did she also know that Addison felt like a girl? Did Addison show early signs? Addison was desperate to connect to a certain trans narrative that didn't quite fit. Her mom said, "Addison, you are looking for answers to questions that don't need to be asked. Who cares? Everything's fine. You are who you are. I love you."

It felt like a relief.

It was the community at the dive bar that inspired Addison to find a fitness community as well. She liked running but wanted to move with other people. Running got lonely, and a pole dancing class reminded Addison that she loved community. She started looking for other group fitness opportunities. A friend suggested CrossFit, and Addison had flashbacks to high school. Picturing football players populating the gym waiting to bully her, she said, "No, I don't fit there. I don't know any trans women who do CrossFit."

Addison Googled "Transgender CrossFit" and found images of women being trans, unapologetically strong, and muscular. She joined a gym, but even after actively reaching out to the online CrossFit community, she never found another trans woman with whom to work out.

At work, Addison was stealth (living as her identified gender while not being out as trans). She was not out as a trans woman. She did not want her trans identity to shadow other parts of her identity at work. She wanted a community at CrossFit that felt safe after being stealth all day at work. Compartmentalizing, keeping it separate, was exhausting. She wanted to be an outspoken advocate of trans rights, so being stealth from nine to five felt less and less tolerable. She felt like the world was trying to make trans people disappear, and it was important for her to be on a brave path to staying visible and alive.

A mentor helped Addison quit her job and believe that she could be out as trans and successful. She got a new job as a trans navigator within the health care system. It has been a huge relief to stop hiding and to be not only tolerated at work but given more power and responsibility because she is trans. Addison has come out in style, getting a modeling gig at a mainstream clothing store for their Pride collection, throwing the opening pitch at an MLB Pride night, and wearing a lifting belt that reads "Trans is strong."

Addison started CrossFit and immediately saw how gendered it is. Instead of being labeled by weight, bars are referred to as the men's bar and the women's bar. The workout of the day is divided by gender. The women's workout has a girl's name, and the men's workout has a boy's name. Suggested weights for lifting are always listed in two categories: one for men and one for women, instead of leaving it open for participants to find a weight that feels comfortable for them. There are mixed-gender competitions, but the leaderboard is broken into two genders. "As a trans person coming into that space I was intimidated right off the bat. What if I'm the strongest that day? Are the people looking at this going to be like, 'She shouldn't be with the women. She should be with the men'?"

Addison stopped entering times and weights on the CrossFit leaderboard. It was too stressful. Two years into training, she noticed she liked the lifting portion better than the cardio portion. She had no interest in doing the workouts as quickly as possible. She wanted to slow down and focus on strength, so she decided to try a powerlifting gym.

Powerlifting can often be less gendered than CrossFit. People compete in gender categories, but the categories are broken up by weight. It is not about who lifts the most weight but the most weight compared with their body weight. In the gym, according to Addison, it is just you versus the bar and pushing your body to its edge, regardless of gender.

Addison took to powerlifting right away and was competing almost immediately.

Powerlifting competitions can be intimidating. You are in front of a crowd and you try to lift as much weight as you can. Once. It is a pass/fail event. Before Addison walked out for her first competitive lift, she turned her focus inward and took deep breaths. The room was loud, but all she could hear was the voice in her head. In front of the crowd, she set her feet and focused her gaze above the heads in the crowd. Everything became quiet, and she did what she came to do.

"As soon as I go to initiate that pull, every single muscle in my body is tense and active, and that feeling is so addicting. When people are like, 'Oh, you were born in the wrong body,' it's like, 'No, the fuck I wasn't. Look at what this body has done for me. Look at what I can do with this body.' I refuse to allow myself to be limited by this idea of 'My body needs to change in order for it to be authentic.' Absolutely not. I give the middle finger to [that] narrative. This body can do incredible things. This culture is the problem. My body is limitless."

Addison's coach pulled her aside after her first competitive lift and said, "I could see you going to that place of just you and the platform. Make sure you don't forget how to do that. That's going to be very important."

Addison broke her goal of deadlifting 300 pounds. Her new goal is 350, which will be double her body weight.

In powerlifting, Addison has found community. In between lifts, she loves to hang with the other lifters and eat junk food, pumping each other up. Like the dive bar, it has become a place that feels like home, like safety, where she belongs just as she is.

Addison lifts for herself. It's not about winning or beating other people. It is about seeing what her body can do and crushing her goals. It's about not being afraid to walk into a weight room, taking up space. In the weight room, she never needs to defend her existence.

Bodies are complicated. Our sex is complicated, and so are hormones, competitive advantage, and athletic performance. Trans women are not men, and trans men engaging with gender-affirming hormone treatment are not doping. Although drawing a line to separate bodies into two neat sex categories is impossible, sport decision-makers are still trying, in the name of fairness. Banning trans athletes from competing will not make drawing that line any more possible or make our sports system more inclusive or fair. And in every attempt to draw that line, it is cis women and intersex, nonbinary, and trans folks who feel the brunt of the gender policing.

Focusing on the unfairness of trans women competing in the female category distracts us from having better conversations about fairness in sports, such as those that address social class and who has access to opportunities in sports. We must distinguish between different kinds of sports, ages, and levels. We must include trans boys and men and not clump them with trans girls and women. We must talk about more than testosterone levels and sex organs. To be a great athlete, it helps to have physical characteristics that are beneficial to your sport, but that is not enough. You also must work hard and compete well. Things like financial stability, emotional stability, good nutrition, good coaching, access to good facilities, and a supportive family help athletes perform well and are totally outside the scope of being cis or trans. There is a reason that sports that require expensive facilities, such as hockey and ice skating, have historically been disproportionately white. Let's talk about fairness, yes. Let's have a conversation about redistributing money in our national sports system so that no kid has to pay to play.

We should all ask more interesting questions about fairness, learn more about testosterone and competitive advantage, and work to create policies that celebrate how nuanced and complex human bodies and sports are. And when we do, we should keep athletes like Ciara, Rhea, Lennox, Al, Jaime, Starlet, and Addison in mind.

3

Are Trans Athletes Dangerous?

Myth: *Trans Athletes Are Doing Harm*

CONSERVATIVE LAWMAKERS AND ANTI-TRANS ADVOCATES argue that trans women must be kept out of public spheres, including sports competitions and locker rooms, because trans women are the same as cis men who aim to do harm. The alleged harm that they seek to prevent comes in two forms. One, that it is dangerous for trans and cis women to compete against each other in contact sports, implying that trans women are bigger and stronger than cis women, which mitigates physical safety.[1] The second is that trans women are predators trying to access spaces like the women's locker room to sexually assault or harass women.[2] In both cases, these narratives are unfounded and inaccurate. The narratives are harmful to trans women, as they perpetuate a myth that trans women are dangerous. The narratives are also dangerous to cis women, as the unfounded panic is leading to more sanctioned policing of women's bodies and women's sports spaces.

Sport has been unsafe, and often violent, since its inception as a professionalized system in the United States (namely, when President Theodore Roosevelt pushed the NCAA to promote American football to encourage boys to be more masculine, killing nineteen athletes in 1905 alone). More recently, we've seen hundreds of girls unequivocally and systemically sexually assaulted in gymnastics. We've seen boys' brains physically damaged in American football. And lately, we've seen trans kids who don't fit neatly into the checkboxes of girl or boy harassed, pushed out of socially supportive spaces, and even victimized by death threats, all for playing sports.

Various forms of violence against cis boys, cis girls, and trans kids raises the question: How can we change sports so that such violence is as unacceptable as it is in, say, schools? A grand question, to be certain, but one with a simple response: We need to create a culture in sports where all athletes are safe and where people can speak out if they are not. The current sociopolitical violence against trans athletes provides an opportunity to reimagine sports culture—to change it to be better, safer, and more inclusive. Reimagining starts with interrogating how violence in sports is dealt with differently depending on gender.

For cis boys and men playing sports, violent collisions are not only accepted but celebrated and expected.[3] A similar collision between two cis women is deemed an accident or unseemly. Take, as a case in point, comments from WNBA announcers and spectators in 2024 about the playing styles of athletes like Caitlin Clark and Angel Reese.[4] A collision between a cis woman and a trans woman is considered dangerous. Underlying these inconsistencies is the belief that there is an innate difference between cis men and women athletes—that cis women need protection because their bodies are naturally weaker. If this were the case, then there are several flaws with the enactment of anti-trans policies.

For instance, in the majority of sports in which women (and men) compete, there are no policies that regulate height, weight, or strength. Yet, many of the points made about the safety of cis women contend that trans women are taller, bigger, and stronger. But, cis women, like trans women, come in all shapes, sizes, and levels of athleticism.[5] If no policy currently exists to regulate height, weight, and strength, there is also no basis for safety concerns.[6]

This also raises questions about men's sport. While the policies are based on the belief that it is unsafe for cis girls and women to compete with trans girls and women, the safety of cis men competing with trans men and nonbinary athletes is not often discussed in those same policies. No measures are in place to protect trans boys and men from cis boys and men athletes because the threat to their safety is deemed insignificant. There are also no measures in place to protect trans men. This is odd because if cis women athletes need to be protected from trans women athletes, then, according to that logic, trans men athletes would need to be protected from cis men athletes. If policies are being written in the name of protecting athletes, wouldn't there also be restrictions against trans men competing?

Such policies (or lack thereof) work together to simultaneously erase and demonize trans athletes, with trans men rendered invisible and trans women portrayed as dangerous social deviants. Politicians use these tropes to justify excluding trans people from sports and health care, while conveniently presenting themselves as protectors of cis girls and women in sports.[7] Lawmakers' assertion that there is a need for the regulation of trans women athletes leads to the regulation, and policing, of all women's bodies.

Since the inception of elite sports organizations in the late eighteenth century, sports organizers have tried to categorize athletes based on sex but have consistently failed to do so.[8] Categorizing has often harmed athletes, especially women athletes.[9] For as long as there has been a female category in sports, women athletes have been screened, ostracized, and violated in the name of preventing (mostly male) athletes from doping and of verifying eligibility.[10]

Official sex verification testing began as early as the 1948 Olympics when athletes competing in the female category were required to bring documentation from their doctors to *prove* they were women.[11] By 1966, the notes from doctors were no longer considered sufficient, so on-site doctor panels were instituted to visually inspect parts of women athletes' bodies, sometimes referred to as *nude parades*.[12] Pushback against the horrific and intrusive nature of the nude parades led to its replacement with a chromosomal-testing method (called Barr body), which was employed on the athletes for the 1968 Olympic games. The Barr body test uses "the presence of an inactive X chromosome . . . as presumed evidence of a Y chromosome"; women with an inactive X chromosome were considered male and ineligible to compete in the women's category.[13]

Not only does the Barr body test invade privacy, but it is ultimately ineffective because it does not acknowledge intersex people—those born with reproductive or sexual anatomy that does not fit into neat male or female categories. In 1 in about 1,500 births, a baby's genitalia are atypical enough to call in a specialist.[14] The number of people with visible and/or subtler sex variations constitutes, by some estimates, up to 1.7 percent of the population.[15]

From 1968 to 1998, the IOC and other sports governing bodies used chromosomal testing for all female competitors.[16] Athletes were tested and given a card that verified their sex. If an athlete could not produce this card, their eligibility was questioned (not unlike, say, apartheid passes). Notably, only athletes competing in the female category have been subjected to sex-verification testing. Male athletes have never had to undergo sex-verification testing, making sex testing one of the primary ways sports governing bodies police gender.[17] Because of human variance, and because this test reduces sex to one chromosomal characteristic, the Barr body testing was later dismissed.

By 1999, formal sex verification was dropped by the IOC, but women athletes' bodies continued to be regulated. After nude parades and chromosome testing, sports governing bodies went on to use hormone levels—testosterone, specifically—to regulate women's sport.

Variance and complexity of the chromosomes and hormones we all possess make it complicated to maintain and regulate any completely female or male category of sport. Caster Semenya, a South African runner, was forced to undergo invasive sex-verification testing and to take suppressants for naturally occurring testosterone in her body.[18]

Compare Semenya to Pedro Spajari, a cis male swimmer from Brazil. In 2016, Spajari was discovered to have Klinefelter syndrome (instead of having XY chromosomes, he has XXY chromosomes). Klinefelter syndrome reduced the levels of his natural testosterone, inhibiting his performance, and so he began testosterone supplementation via hormone replacement therapy. His treatments were approved by the IOC and World Aquatics, and he has since gone on to compete in multiple Olympic and world swimming competitions without issue.[19] Having low testosterone levels made him weaker and less competitive, spurring international governing bodies to support his hormone replacement therapy so that he might be more competitive. Having a natural amount of testosterone for Semenya made her theoretically too strong and competitive, spurring international governing bodies to demand hormone replacement therapy to make her weaker and less competitive. Many scholars, activists, and athletes question why we are regulating the female category of sports and not the male category.[20]

There has never been a reported case of a trans woman assaulting a cis woman in a locker room. Moreover, there are no known instances of sexual assault perpetrated by a trans woman against a cis woman in sport. Conversely, trans women are often extremely vulnerable in such spaces because of the growing anti-trans sentiment. In fact, many trans athletes, instead of doing harm in locker rooms, avoid locker rooms so they themselves don't get harmed.

The assumption that trans athletes, particularly trans women, pose a danger to cis women in bathrooms and locker rooms is both pervasive and baseless. This narrative, which purports that sexual predators will exploit gender nondiscrimination laws to sneak into private women's spaces (like locker rooms), has been consistently debunked by experts and empirical studies as not only baseless but "beyond specious."[21] Several studies affirm "there is no current evidence that granting transgender individuals access to gender-corresponding restrooms results in an increase in sexual offenses."[22] Research shows that trans people are far more likely to be harmed in these spaces than to pose a threat to others.

Trans women are frequently subjected to harassment and violence in restrooms and locker rooms. A 2013 survey found that 70 percent of transgender and gender nonconforming respondents reported being denied access, verbally harassed, or physically assaulted in gendered public restrooms.[23] Moreover, the 2015 U.S. Transgender Survey revealed that one in eight trans individuals was verbally harassed, physically attacked, or sexually assaulted while accessing public spaces, with many others avoiding them altogether because of fear of such violence.[24]

For kids, restrictions on restroom access because of gender

identity significantly increased the risk of sexual assault for trans youths, not for cis youths.[25] Further complicating this issue is the harassment faced by cisgender women who are mistaken as trans and are similarly targeted.[26] The logic of barring trans people from women's spaces not only fails to protect cis women but also actively endangers trans and nonbinary people and athletes.

The argument that trans women should be excluded from cis women's sport spaces on the grounds of safety relies on the unfounded presumption that men are inherently dangerous and women are inherently safe. Such views ignore the fact that just as some cis women commit acts of sexual violence, they are not universally barred from public spaces.[27] To apply a different standard to trans women, absent supporting evidence, is nothing short of discriminatory.

Avery, a trans woman who was raised as a boy and played boys' hockey, never showered after the games in hopes of avoiding the bullying that happened in the locker rooms. Skipping showers or showering with boxers on came with their own flavors of harassment. Avery made a traveling team but quit and joined recreational hockey because they were so sick of the bullying. Of course, quitting the team welcomed harassment for a few weeks, too. They couldn't win.

Avery began their transition when they were twenty-eight. They saw a counselor once a month for five or six years and paid $120 per session out of pocket. Insurance didn't cover it, so it was an expensive investment in their well-being. "I was really full of a lot of shame and a lot of internal hate and transphobia myself. I couldn't even say the words."

Now, as a trans woman playing recreational softball on a mix-gender team, just getting out there and playing feels like overcoming their fears week in and week out. Avery speaks to the disconnect between all the anti-trans hate they see on social media, coupled with all the policies banning trans athletes, and what a fantastic time they have playing softball out in public. "And all it takes is getting out there and meeting people and they're going to see that I'm not really that different than they are. I'm not a pervert. I'm not a groomer. I'm not a sexual predator."

Sports and movement can help trans athletes take a break from the angst that comes with navigating a gender that is different from their sex assigned at birth and the social consequences of being trans. For example, when Ciara, a trans woman runner, came out to her partner, her partner asked her to move out immediately, which meant leaving her three kids as well. Ciara used running as a way to regulate her feelings. Running also gave Ciara an identity. When she ran, she was a runner. Period. "I've had so many days where I just can't stand to look at myself in the mirror. But once I strap on the trainers and head out, I don't see that anymore. I just feel the way my body is moving. I've always loved that sensation of just really flying over the rocks and roots and stuff. Just making it go. That always makes me feel better about my body and about myself, even on those days when I can't stand to look in the mirror."

It took her a while to dress how she wanted around her kids

because she did not want to shock them. "It did cause some dysphoria and bad feelings because I was not being honest with them. I rationalized that I was trying to ease things along for them. In the end, I got there. Now they see me in my pink fuzzy bathrobe. Nobody seems to bat an eye."

Ciara is a recreational athlete. She is not pursuing medals. She doesn't use a locker room. Reading the headlines about banning trans athletes has sent Ciara into a state of mental distress. She knows she is not a monster, as some of the articles make her out to be. "It's like they're trying to make sport itself an androcentric activity because they're making it all about absolute achievement or performance. If you're in the Olympics, that's a real concern. But most sports that happens is not the Olympics. Yes, I play sports. Yes, I was assigned male at birth. Yes, I went through male puberty. And yes, I definitely have some advantages because of that. But I am not in the Olympics. I am not hammering everybody around me. I'm getting my ass beat constantly. Let me play. That's how I feel about it."

These harmful false narratives that trans athletes are dangerous in collisions and in the locker room pave the way for restrictive state policies, reinterpretations of federal laws, and new regulations by sports governing bodies, all aimed at trans athletes. Cultural conversations combined with politically controlled sports spaces make it nearly impossible for trans athletes to function as full citizens. In sidelining them, everyone misses out.

One antidote to slow the perpetuation of the harmful myths

about trans athletes and dismember the tropes is to hear from the trans athletes themselves. Finley is a trans woman who, instead of doing harm, was a young athlete who needed protection.

The first time Finley picked up a tennis racket, she was seven. In that very first moment, she knew without a doubt that tennis would save her life.

Finley grew up in what she described as a "low-level cult." Her family moved around a lot, but Detroit was a homebase of sorts. It was there that Finley picked up her mom's tennis racket and started hitting a ball against a giant brick wall across from her apartment complex. She loved it right away and spent hours by herself smashing the ball against the wall.

Even with glass on the ground, it was where she went to feel safe. She was a gender nonconforming kid in the 1970s in a rough area of Detroit, in the context of a homophobic community. Before school, after school, all summer, she hit the ball against the wall. When they moved across the country and across the world, she would find a wall to hit a tennis ball against.

Finley was also the kid who got beat up on the playground for being gender nonconforming. She dealt with being bullied by isolating as much as possible. When she was young, she'd take the bus to the art museum to get a break from her community. The museum felt like home. There were a few adults over the years who saw her and looked after her. A kind older woman approached Finley and simply said, "I see you" in a way that made her feel seen and safe. There was also a college student at the tennis club who checked in on her and talked to her about music. He felt safe to her, and she always played better when he was around.

Eventually, her family settled back in Detroit for a few years in a building closer to a tennis court, and Finley hit against a backboard there. She was so good, eventually people just invited her to play with them, delighted with her intensity. "I'm violently competitive," she said. "I want to win, and I am going to shred the fur off a tennis ball to do it." Even before she picked up a tennis racket, Finley's dad put her in a wrestling tournament. She didn't like wrestling, but when she understood it was a competition, she clenched her jaw and won the whole thing. With tennis, she got good fast and started competing around age ten in a twelve-and-under league. She strung rackets and coached kids—anything to make enough money to pay for lessons and tournament entry fees.

With money always tight, Finley believed a tennis scholarship was her only path to college. When the time came, at age seventeen, she broke her femur in a tournament. In surgery, the doctor found a cyst in her femur and regrafted it. She almost lost her leg. The injury was serious enough to put an end to her tennis career and scholarship hopes.

As a kid, Finley remembers being mesmerized by fully decked-out cyclists training around the lakes. She used the money she made from teaching tennis to buy a bike, and cycling became not only rehab but her next obsession as well.

In her hometown, there was a scholar who was recruiting folks for an eight-month cycling study. He recruited Finley, so

she got access to a regimented training program, regular testing, and high-level coaching. Her competitive nature took over,
and she was hooked, entering rigorous road races almost right
away. She loved racing and couldn't get enough. She said, "I
don't know if the sport mattered so much as just the competition. I just loved being competitive."

Finley moved overseas to get access to more races and entered
about eighty a year. In Europe, she got good at racing in big
packs and narrow roads. She learned how to hide in a pack and
handle herself in the thick of a race. "Time trials always felt
like these one-off poems I wrote with my legs and lungs and
heart, finding the edge of what my body could do, and some-
how willing it to do more."

Back in the 1980s, amateur cyclists could make a sizable
amount of money winning races. In addition to those earnings,
Finley was offered a cycling scholarship. She got her university
scholarship after all.

Finley transitioned in her late forties. In her mind, that was
late. When laws started changing around informed consent
and transitioning without a long trial period, Finley started to
know that was the path forward but was convinced it was not
the time socially or economically. She avoided thinking about
transitioning, always reluctant about who she was, always hoping she was not trans, always wishing it would magically disappear from her plate.

It never did.

Those years of waiting were hard and dark. She was
unhoused for three years, which was grueling, exhausting, and

scary. Feeling unstable, she couldn't imagine adding a gender transition to the mix, and she didn't have the money. There were moments in that season when Finley could put thoughts of transition so far on the back burner that she forgot about it, believing it would never truly become a realistic option. Despair set in. She lost her job, didn't know how to go on, and attempted suicide. She knew her choice was to transition or end her life. "I don't like that kind of all-or-nothing sort of attitude," she said, "but that's really where I was."

Eventually, her competitiveness came through again, and Finley hustled from the streets into a job that made real money. With stable funding, transitioning felt like an option. It was a rocky road, but as soon as she started the transition, she felt relief and thought, "I should have done this a long time ago." Not being in a queer community, she simply didn't know the pathway until it appeared.

She couldn't articulate it at the time, but now, Finley can clearly see that her determination and commitment to tennis and then cycling was about having power and safety inside her body. There was something so soothing about getting into a flow state. She could shut everything else out and have a singular focus of winning one point. Then the next. Then the next. Or cycling one mile. Then the next. Then the next.

Both tennis and cycling are like chess. There is raw skill and thinking and maneuvering, or "weaseling," as Finley put it. She always pushed her body to the edge, and her competitive spirit set her apart. "And it's a matter of being able to read the terrain, read the wind conditions, read the heat, and also, then, read what one's body can do and just be able to go for it."

After Finley started to transition, she realized that when she plays, the white noise falls away. "I was self-medicating all these years. I like to say I chose my drugs wisely. I chose sports. Sports and competition gave me agency over my body. It's how I survived before transition." Pretransition, she was driven by angst and anger. She was playing to work out her rage. She was playing to stay alive. There was an urgency and a clinging to it. Now that she has settled into her body and her identity, the anger has fallen away. Now, she is less focused on the outcome and can enjoy moving her body in space for the pure love of it.

Finley won her first club tennis tournament in the women's category a few years back. "Didn't drop a set," she said. "I'd trade everything I won pretransition for this one." The win was a turning point that no one could ever take away from her. It wasn't about the medal; it was about what it stood for. She was here in her body, playing, and she had to fight damn hard for all of that. "Sport feels like a luxury at this point in my life, and the fact that I get to play at all is a gift."

Finley is an artist and works in set design. She speaks of sports in artistic terms too. Tennis and cycling were opportunities for her to "draw with one's body and space." Painting and sports feel like one and the same to her. She took her love of drawing and painting and used it to move her body through space in a brilliant and beautiful way. An artist and an athlete both sacrifice and pay attention to detail in ways that Finley respects and lives out.

Sports, for Finley, is a form of self-expression. It seems unbearably cruel to restrict any opportunity for healthy self-expression for a kid or an adult making her way in the world.

Something clicked when Finley picked up a tennis racket. Sports was an arena for Finley to metabolize her angst and anger. It was a place to focus her competitiveness on something constructive. It was an opportunity to take a break from the world and be safe in her body moving. It kept her alive until the white noise fell away, and she could enjoy simply being. She knows the road ahead with governing bodies writing restrictions is going to be bumpy. She is clear that any child who wants to express themselves through playing a sport should be able to, and she hopes her story can be considered in the conversation.

Using any metric, it is extremely dangerous to be a trans woman in America. Finley's dark season is a sobering reminder of the inner angst and sense of isolation that can come with navigating a trans identity in a decidedly cis-centered society. The external pressure to conform can be oppressive, and the consequences can be dire. The murder rate for Black trans women, for example, is five times higher than the murder rate for the general population. The folks who told their stories as part of this project articulated feeling an ever-present danger in myriad ways. A refrain was the exhaustion that comes with moving through society being constantly vigilant, looking for signs of danger. For some, playing sports is a pause in the vigilance, a respite, an oasis. While playing, they can drop into their bodies and be safe there. For others, the white noise doesn't fall away like it did for Finley. The white noise continues. The very real and perceived threats remain a barrier to easeful play for other trans athletes.

While trans women like Finley fight for their mental health, the assumption that trans women are physically dangerous toward their cis opponents is effectively frothing the moral panic. Take Fallon Fox, the first openly trans woman mixed martial arts (MMA) fighter. In 2014, during a match, Fox fractured her opponent's orbital bone, an injury common in mixed martial arts. Yet in media coverage, this incident became a weapon to stoke fears of physical harm: "Fairness aside, this is dangerous. Recall that thanks to his male strength, trans MMA fighter Fallon Fox cracked a female opponent's skull in 2014," wrote Ramona Tausz in a piece for the *New York Post* in 2021. What Tausz conveniently leaves out is that Fox broke her opponent's orbital bone, which is not uncommon, regardless of gender; between 2001 and 2020, over 73 percent of MMA fights resulted in some form of eye injury, with 17 percent of those involving orbital fractures.[28]

Still, in the article, Tausz used "his" and "male" on purpose, denying Fox's transness and implying unfairness, but then going to danger. The implication? That Fox's body, because it was once categorized as male, was inherently violent. Curiously, when cis men collide on the field or in the ring, we call it sport. But when a trans woman like Fox steps into that same arena, the narrative changes. The emphasis is no longer on the competitive nature of the sport but on the supposed threat she poses. By selectively presenting facts, Tausz created a narrative that focused on the supposed danger trans women pose without acknowledging the risks trans women themselves face, both in sports and in society at large.

This narrative relies on several problematic assumptions. First, it assumes that trans women have the same social privileges that cis men have, suggesting that they enter competition with an unfair advantage rooted in bodily strength. It is built on a simplistic idea that "male" bodies are always stronger than "female" bodies, ignoring the vast variation in human bodies, regardless of gender. This trope implies that trans women's bodies are inherently male, ignoring their gender identity and lived experiences. It also suggests that trans women, unlike cis men, need to be policed in sports, as though they pose an inherent threat. This feeds into a broader societal fear that trans women are deceptive or manipulative, particularly in competitive spaces like sports.

One striking example of this belief can be seen in the rhetoric of Republican Senator Mike Lee, who argued "biological males [that is, trans women] might [transition] to win a prize or a trophy or scholarship. Others might do it just to prove that they can or for bragging rights. Others still might do it in a deliberate, sadistic effort to harm girls."[29]

This narrative is not only misleading but also deeply harmful. It paints trans women as manipulative figures willing to exploit systems for personal gain—a notion that does not align with the lived realities of trans athletes. If we listen to the stories of trans athletes, we find not deception or malice but a deep longing to live in and move in their bodies. Trans athletes are not transitioning to win prizes but to compete in ways that feel right for them. This desire for authenticity is far more nuanced and humane than the fear-based portrayals offered by critics of trans athletes. And navigating the world as a trans person can feel unsafe, as Peter and Robyn describe.

Peter said that after a childhood of feeling free and secure in his body, where he dressed and did things that were probably coded as masculine, puberty hit. Peter described it as a terror. The thought crossed his mind, "Well, if I could just wake up and be a boy tomorrow, I would do it. Sure." Yet he had no concept of transitioning as an option. It was just a misalignment that he thought he had to endure. It can be helpful to think about what your body can do as opposed to what it looks like when managing dysphoria; diving into sports kept Peter's dark thoughts and self-hatred at bay. He had no idea that he was trans, and looking back, he thinks it could have been crushing to have to leave women's lacrosse. Now playing as a trans man, Peter sees potential for sports to be an empowering place but does not consider sports safe. He is misgendered in co-ed spaces and called derogatory names in men's leagues. Even if these moments happen less and less often, the threat is always there.

Robyn is a trans girl who clearly articulates her desire for authenticity and her desire to play and keep playing. She talks back to the myth that she is dangerous and must be sidelined. It is a child's full-time job to play. Playing is good for your brain and your body development. It feeds creativity and agency. Play allows a child to be a child. Robyn, being a trans kid, had to grow up too fast with not enough access to play.

Robyn stopped cutting her hair at age four. She started using she/her pronouns at five and changed her name at six. When she was seven, while some of her peers were in the bliss of

playing soccer unencumbered, she was at her state's capitol tes-
tifying on her own behalf.

"When we were playing, I would be the mom in house, or
the sister, or when we were playing fairies, I would be the queen
of the fairies or the fairy princess. I was always the female, and
all of my friends would use she/her pronouns for me, and I
loved it. I had three main best friends, and they all were super
supportive; their parents were supportive. We are all still best
friends to this day."

As a child who is trans, Robyn's play has been severely limited. When she was in the second grade, Robyn tried to play soccer, but her teammates made her uncomfortable. "There were a
lot of kids I didn't know, and at the time, I was really uncomfortable with kids who I didn't know and kids who didn't really
want to interact with me at all. I would try and interact with
them, and they would just ignore me." She played for two years
before quitting. It was too painful to be excluded.

The isolation was dramatic for Robyn in part because she is
such an extrovert. Her mom said she used to come home crying in the first grade because she only had eight best friends.
She collected introverts around her and welcomed them into
her world. She loved people, got energy from people, and felt
the sting when kids didn't want to be around her because of her
gender expression.

Research shows that sport participation correlates with higher academic performance and lower rates of depression for all
youths, but for trans kids, the opportunity to play sports can be
a matter of life or death.[30] Suicidality is shockingly common,

with almost 44 percent of transgender youths—versus 16 percent of cis youths—reporting having considered suicide in the previous year.[31] Trans youths who have access to a gender-affirming space at school, like a sports team, are 25 percent less likely to report a suicide attempt within a year.[32] But sports can go beyond just supporting mental health. For many even marginally successful athletes, sports create a space for people to push their minds and bodies to an edge where they realize how much they are capable of. Setting goals and achieving them, for example, can grow a sense of agency and help athletes feel, instead of helpless, powerful.

Robyn has been swimming since she was two months old. Her family has a pool in their backyard, and she loves swimming laps with her sister and inviting friends over to beat the heat. She has early memories of swim lessons, playing with Disney Princess swim toys in the water. Robyn joined a swim team in hopes it would go better than soccer. The swim team is where Robyn realized that part of being on a team could be about building community and making friends.

When she was in the third grade, the swim team paused during COVID, and that is when her state started passing bans so that trans athletes couldn't play. Seeing the bans come out was very hard on Robyn. "I felt like I might never be able to play sports again. It was really scary. At the time, I wasn't playing sports on a team, but it was upsetting to know that I didn't actually have the option to do it. I just wasn't able to play sports. So, I would get my energy out by riding bikes with my friends around our neighborhood."

Robyn didn't learn to ride her bike without training wheels until the end of the second grade, but then she wanted to ride all the time. "I liked being able to exercise and look around the neighborhood and explore, and I really like the feeling when you're biking and it's super hot. When you're going super fast, the wind wooshes." She and her dad would bike around the neighborhood, running errands for her mom. When she was younger, she had a bike gang of neighborhood kids. That crew has drifted apart, and now Robyn has two neighborhood friends who will bike with her.

At Robyn's school, a teacher started an informal running club. Kids meet on Mondays after school and run together for a few miles. Because of the sports ban, Robyn can't play on sports teams, so this running club is an outlet for her to move and be. Belonging is a body feel. When you are in a place where you feel like you belong, you can relax. You're in. You don't have to monitor your body. Robyn's coach was giving her a chance to belong on a team. She has a place to go after school and a group of kids with whom to associate. In the ease of belonging, she can grow.

Robyn was open about her transition, and plenty of kids didn't know how to react, and they made her uncomfortable with their avoidance and exclusion. She is no longer vocal about being trans at school. She just tells people she is a girl, which she is. "I remember when I first transitioned, I was very open about my gender identity, but right now, I'm not very open. A lot of people in my school don't really know, and I don't really talk about it much. I talk about LGBTQ rights at school and how it's important, but they don't know that I'm trans."

Some kids at Robyn's school are actively offensive to her face, saying horrible things, and it is scary for her. On a school camping trip, for example, a kid was making fun of being trans and said, "I'm trans, you guys. It's okay if I go shower in the girls' shower with the doors open."

On the bus, the two kids right in front of Robyn were saying things like, "Trans kids playing sports is so unfair. Trans girls have a huge advantage over cis girls." Robyn recounts, "Then they were talking about trans celebrities and misgendering them on purpose. I was crying. I was so uncomfortable, and my teachers don't really understand what it's like."

Already by the age of thirteen, Robyn had been a trans advocate for years. She wants to tell people, "We are something to be celebrated and not something to be feared, and we're just like you, but you're trying to make us seem like we're not. We are actual people who have actual lives."

After starting to show up at the capitol at age seven to testify and returning there again and again, she told her mom, "I'm done going to the capitol and asking for my existence." None of her other classmates fight to play and tell lawmakers how their policies hurt them. They don't have to take time away to tell the adults how to behave better. They don't have to worry about their safety. Robyn does. She reads the articles that make her out to be a monster. She hears the slurs in the hallways and lunchroom. She had a trans friend get pinned by police officers at a protest. As she gets older, she is getting more scared. Robyn arguably needs a team to belong to the most, and in the face of the bans in her state, the informal running club is an oasis.

"A lot of our people around us are moving away because they're really scared, but now people are moving in to where they're living, and they're not educated, and they're not exactly supportive, and it's really scary."

Robyn decided to put her energy into a different type of advocacy. She cofounded Trans Prom with her friend Daniel. Trans Prom is a fully student-led inclusive prom event. They wanted to show that trans and nonbinary kids should be celebrated instead of feared. Kids came from all over the country to dance and celebrate. There was a grand march, a selfie station, and a dance so that trans and nonbinary kids could feel safe, dance, and be kids. She got the idea in February and pulled it off that May. Robyn created the logo, of which she is very proud.

At prom, Robyn could relax and be silly because everyone there supported her. She didn't have to be on high alert and vigilant, looking over her shoulder for the kid who would demean her. It was profoundly simple and deeply necessary. Kids deserve to feel safe, to be kids, to play, and to dance. Robyn said it best. When we asked her what the highlight of Trans Prom was, she said, "I loved dancing with all of my friends."

Robyn is not asking to play in the gender category she is aligned with to win medals or do harm. She just wants people to believe her when she tells them who she is. She was assigned a label at birth based on her external sex organs. Eventually, she came to know that the label didn't fit. It takes an amazing amount of courage and self-knowledge to say, "I am a girl," despite what so many consider biological "proof."

Robyn is not a legal adult, and she is navigating a physical, emotional, and psychological process of coming into her true identity. Often the angst and confusion associated with coming out as trans happen in isolation, as a secret, as a creeping feeling of being different. The prevailing cultural narrative that trans athletes pose some kind of threat harms young trans athletes like Robyn most of all. This fact should be enough to sway sports organizations, schools, and policymakers to change their approach to these restrictive policies.

The myths saying that trans people are dangerous make being trans feel dangerous to trans folks like Robyn. She is watching sports bans and bathroom bills that all claim that she is dangerous and needs to be policed to keep others safe. The sports bans and more general anti-trans bills are creating a landscape that makes it feel very unsafe to be out as trans. Between 2016 and 2018, conservative politicians in North Carolina staged campaigns to prevent trans women from using bathrooms consistent with their gender.[33] The arguments framing this effort cast trans women as predatory, suggesting that any man could claim to be a woman to access women's spaces, like bathrooms, ostensibly to harm or even sexually violate children.[34] It is a manufactured trope that works to justify the policing of and marginalization of trans bodies. This rhetoric mirrors the anti-integration campaigns of the 1950s, in which Black men were depicted as threats to the safety and purity of white women:

> Like black sexuality, trans sexuality (specifically trans women) has been socially purported to be a threat to white womanhood. As trans women do not subscribe to the gender they were assigned at birth, they violate the white supremacist construct of what femininity is to be . . . in addition, they were often depicted as predators, lurking in the shadows to tempt and convert.[35]

Spilling over into sports, this trope wrongly presents trans women athletes as "biological men," who lurk in bathrooms and locker rooms and threaten the purity and safety of cis girls. Such tropes politicize trans and cis women in ways that further white feminine fragility, while pushing legislation that represses trans people collectively.[36]

These fear-based narratives in the media work on several levels. Being trans is something children should fear becoming. Trans people are also something to fear. Trans people have malicious intent in moving and competing. And something must be done to stop trans people.

There is only one group seemingly benefiting from the scrutiny on trans athletes in the media and from the control of trans athletes' bodies via policies: conservative lawmakers, who are gaining power, money, and attention. The moral panic about trans women is being chummed in the name of protecting cis girls, but it is replicating prevailing systems that have historically stymied gender equity in sport.[37]

Politicians often position themselves as moral authorities, claiming to protect their constituents, such as cis women in sports, while presenting themselves as arbiters of social order who are enforcing rules to control perceived deviance for the greater good. The reality, however, is strikingly ironic. When questioned by the Associated Press, many conservative politicians pushing anti-trans bills couldn't even name a single trans athlete in their states.[38] Trans athletes become faceless scapegoats, mere symbols in a broader moral panic, while public opinion against them rises.[39]

Politicians acting as moral entrepreneurs (those who both fuel and regulate moral panic) would have the public believe that trans women and girls are a threat to gender equity in sports. In an opinion piece for the *Altoona Mirror*, Nancy Neuman wrote, "Are we willing to deny girls the opportunity to compete equally against other girls in sports? Are we willing to turn a blind eye to all the girls, especially minority girls, who will be robbed of scholarships because of unfair competitions against transgender athletes?"[40]

Neuman's rhetoric claims a moral duty to protect women athletes, excluding trans women. This is a familiar contradiction in politics; the same politicians who claim to be defending women's sports were opponents of Title IX and gender equity.[41] They have long resisted efforts to improve opportunities for women in sports, particularly for women of color.[42]

Now, these politicians are positioning themselves as protectors, using trans athletes to push broader agendas that limit bodily autonomy for all women and girls, including their right to fully participate in sports. This strategy promotes fear and division and obscures the real challenges facing women's sports and the broader fight for gender equity.

In sports, women and girls face such serious challenges as unequal opportunities, inequitable funding, pay gaps, gender-stereotyped media coverage, limited sponsorship opportunities, higher rates of sexual harassment and abuse, and inadequate implementation of gender-equality policies.[43] These are genuine threats that deserve our attention. There have been many attempts to address these threats that include fighting for athletic opportunities, combating sexual assault, campaigning for quality media coverage, and demanding representation in leadership.[44] Yet, anti-trans activists who claim to protect women's sports have not engaged in these efforts in meaningful ways.[45] Instead, they manipulate the narrative of "protecting" women's sports to justify excluding trans women.

Sports offer profound social, physical, and mental benefits, particularly for children in key developmental years.[46] In the United States, nearly 70 percent of children aged six to twelve participate in athletics.[47] Through sports, they learn critical life skills, like communication, teamwork, and leadership, and they build strong peer connections.[48] Girls who have access to sports report better grades, improved health, higher self-esteem, fewer risky behaviors, and stronger confidence in their abilities.[49] Why would we deny any child these benefits? Trans youths like Robyn, navigating their identity within a rigid binary system, may need the community and support of sports more than most kids.

Sports participation can also foster cohesion and increase understanding across different social groups.[50] Interpersonal relationships between cis and trans people can build empathy and acceptance, significantly reducing prejudice and transphobia.[51] Denying trans youths access to sports harms not only them but also their cis peers by preventing these opportunities for connection and mutual understanding.

One group harmed by anti-trans narratives is cis boys.[52] A recent study found that hypermasculine, anti-LGBTQ language pervades youth sports environments, particularly boys' sports.[53] This "locker room talk" often includes homophobic, transphobic, and misogynistic slurs aimed at enforcing traditional masculinity, with phrases like "man up." Such toxic language harms cis boys as well as LGBTQ youths. Ironically, straight white boys, who are often seen as benefiting from this system, experience the greatest decline in self-esteem because of this culture of policing masculinity.[54]

Ultimately, the culture of exclusion and toxic masculinity in sports undermines the mental health of all kids involved, regardless of gender. The solution lies not in restricting participation but in making sports more inclusive. By allowing all children, cis and trans alike, to access the benefits of sports, we foster healthier, more empathetic environments that empower all athletes, challenge outdated gender norms, and create a path toward equity in sports.

Anti-trans bans are creating a landscape that feels unsafe for trans athletes to be out. Arguably, the landscape feels the most unsafe for trans women like Phoenix and CeCé who are excelling at their sports.

Phoenix is a trans woman sprinter. Phoenix's adults, as she calls them, believed in conversion therapy. From an early age, Phoenix could not articulate that she was a trans girl, but she did know she had to hide whatever she was from her parents.

The hiding was so intense and brought on so much panic that Phoenix had breathing issues as a kid. She didn't feel safe in her body, at home, or with peers. She lived in survival mode. Boys on her teams picked fights with her for being queer; she took the bait and often ended up severely battered. Phoenix tried swimming, excelled at it, and was on her way to the Olympic Development Program in the backstroke event. But her success felt dirty. She didn't feel like herself competing as a boy. She used her success as her only retort to kids ridiculing her gender expression. She longed to compete as herself, in the women's category. Even now, as an adult, Phoenix contends with gender dysphoria and anorexia every morning.

Like Phoenix, CeCé is a trans woman runner who is incredibly fast. She is Black, beautiful, powerful, and fierce. Much of society's underexplored and unresolved feelings, curiosities, and angst lands unfairly on her body.

CeCé was born happy. It was her nature to be kind and positive, sharing her smile everywhere she went. She was so happy, in fact, her family got annoyed. As early as age four, they told her to be more aggressive, fearing that people would take advantage of her. They worried she was too kind, too happy. CeCé didn't know that was possible.

Instead of becoming more aggressive, she doubled down and stayed true to herself. As a child, CeCé already sensed something was different inside of her. "I had to overcompensate in other areas just to make sure that I'm being the best person I can be. In return, hopefully, they'll see me as a human being, and they won't bully me or treat me bad."

CeCé grew up in Jamaica, and she reflected on how that culture influenced gender roles: "Men go to work. They earn money and bring it back home. Women stay at home, wash the clothes, take care of the kids, cook, and clean. They make sure there's food on the table when the man gets home."

There were social consequences for acting outside of gender norms. Men who wore tight clothes or clear nail polish were harassed and assumed gay. It was not okay to be gay, and you could "prove" you weren't gay by getting married to a woman and having children. Girls could be tomboys, which was more acceptable than being an effeminate man. During CeCé's childhood in Jamaica, it was not an option to be trans.

CeCé's family pushed stereotypically masculine items on her. They bought her oversized clothes to hide her feminine physique. If she crossed her legs, wore tight clothes, or leaned against the wall the wrong way, she'd get a slap from one of her aunts: "Stop that. Boys don't do that." They wanted her to play cricket and soccer, climb trees and bike, get cuts and scrapes and bruises. CeCé wanted to dance and sing. She wanted to play with Barbies and cheerlead. She asked for a doll, and got an action figure. She resigned to acting gender neutral because she didn't identify as a boy, and she couldn't identify as a girl. Her mom told her, "Your skin is too clear and smooth for a boy. You have to rough yourself up and get some scars." The next day, she bought CeCé a bike, and, inevitably, CeCé fell and did start getting scraped up. She masked her true self to stay safe, but that couldn't change who she was on the inside.

"I just wanted to be happy and free, but I felt like they kept pushing me to be an aggressive boy." It was no better in school. "The kids bullied me. They constantly asked me if I was a girl or a boy, and those were the nice ones." CeCé, unpacking the bullying, said, "The only people who give me a hard time are boys because, I don't know, maybe they feel some sort of sexual attraction towards me and how I carry myself." She noticed race playing a role, saying, "I was mostly targeted by Black boys, Black men, and Black people, like, 'Oh, here's somebody like me who is going outside of the cultural norms. That's fucked up. Why do you have to put this on our people?'"

CeCé ran track through childhood and tried volleyball and tennis. She loved American tennis stars and sisters Venus and Serena Williams and emulated Jamaican sprinters Veronica Campbell Brown and Shelly-Ann Fraser-Pryce. While being raised as a boy, she wanted to be like the women stars. CeCé wanted to play netball, a sport like basketball that her mom and aunt played, but she couldn't because it was a woman's sport. She loved the physique she developed from playing volleyball, tennis, and running track. Being good at sports gained her respect.

"I loved that sports didn't pick and choose who deserved to go to the next level or go farther. That was solemnly determined in how good the person was and how hard they worked. Athletes have the ability to really change the world and change people's mind, perceptions, narrative."

When CeCé was in the fifth grade, she did well at her school's field day and was chosen to represent her school in a sprint relay at the National Stadium against the other schools in Jamaica. Olympians Usain Bolt and Fraser-Pryce were there. When CeCé stepped into that stadium, she thought, "I am going to be an Olympian. This is for me. This is where I belong. I'm going to represent my country."

In high school volleyball, CeCé had a female coach who looked out for her. She wouldn't let CeCé's teammates bully her or be rude to her. She remembers that competing against all-boys schools was always a little scary. She sat next to her coach on the bus and stuck close to her as they entered the school. People stared. CeCé wore her uniform tight and showed off her feminine legs. She didn't fit in. She never had any friends on her teams but still played because she loved the game. She was so good, her teammates put up with her so they could win. CeCé couldn't deny she was different from the boys, and that difference felt dangerous: "It was really hard to express myself in an authentic way in Jamaica because the truth of it is that I could have lost my life. Like people would have just deemed me ineligible to live. I couldn't make any wrong moves; I had to make sure that I catch the bus on time and not be alone after dark."

When CeCé was sixteen, her mom found out she was Skyping with a boy and pulled a machete on her. Her mom's husband stepped between them to calm his wife down and make sure CeCé didn't get hurt. He put CeCé's mom in the car and drove away, leaving CeCé alone in the house. They didn't answer her calls. They didn't come back for five days.

CeCé lied to her mom when they came home, saying she thought she was bisexual but now it was clear she was straight, and she would only date women. "I was scared for my life," she said. "To hear your mom tell you this every single day that if you turn out to be a 'battyman' or a 'faggot,' she's going to kill you. Obviously, you're going to not be who you are."

Moving hundreds of miles away for college in New Hampshire felt like an escape. With the distance, CeCé could finally be herself. She moved through the world, and started to compete in track and field, as a woman. The distance from home provided a thin sense of security. Even if her mom found out, CeCé calculated that she had six hours until her mom could get to her.

The NCAA policy at that time allowed trans women to compete if they had been on testosterone suppressants for a year or longer. CeCé was compliant, and her testosterone levels were lower than the NCAA's threshold and that of some of her cis female opponents. CeCé's hormone treatment was aggressive and had severe consequences on her body. Her dosage is way higher than that of a typical trans person who is not an elite athlete. She felt depleted but wanted to make sure her hormone levels didn't restrict her from competing, where she had to show her hormone levels in a range the NCAA deemed normal for the female category.

Being a Black trans woman is nothing short of exhausting. "Black women are constantly being compared to men. The fact that I'm tall, I'm athletic, it just throws people off. And then once they know the fact that I am trans, it's just like, 'There it is. I always knew.'" Every doctor CeCé has gone to has told her she is their first trans patient. This matters for so many reasons, one of which is that she was trying to get cleared to compete in the NCAA. If they forgot to log one appointment, it could have thrown off her progress. She often feels like her doctors don't take her seriously. They expect her to act like an angry Black woman. She *is* livid, but she refuses to show it because it is what they are expecting.

In college, CeCé won a lot, but it never felt like winning because she received so much hate and discrimination. She got nervous showing up at meets after receiving threats, worried she would be attacked or shot. "For me, that is a whole other mental health ball game going into competition knowing that people are going to target my crotch, looking for that affirmation and policing me in that way."

Gender-affirming surgery is expensive, is often not covered by insurance, and has huge physical consequences.[55] Choosing not to undergo gender-affirming surgery also has consequences. Tucking and binding can be painful for some trans athletes.[56] Ripping, tearing, bleeding, and severe pain can happen from binding and tucking; it can also affect confidence. CeCé doesn't identify with some of her body parts and doesn't want to think about them. Could she have been even faster without the physical restriction and mental strife?

CeCé ran her races and then tried to stay out of the public's eye. It was either hide or fight, and she knew fighting would get her in trouble and endanger her ability to run. "What I control is how I present myself to the world and how I show up." But the reality is that showing up at races and in the weight room in a sports bra and spandex shorts is scary. It is not harming others but CeCé clearly articulates how transphobia contributes to her feeling unsafe.

Every time CeCé enters a room, a restaurant, or the gym, heads turn. People try to figure out who she is and how to classify her. When she is wearing tight track clothes, she notices people looking between her legs. She hears other athletes and coaches talking about her. They think she is too tall and too muscular to compete as a woman. She doesn't live up to what other people think a woman is. She doesn't believe being born a woman is a necessary criterion.

While CeCé battles body and gender dysphoria, feeling like her mental state and physical state are at war, she does not feel safe in society. Her internal and external life, then, both feel threatening. Alone in her apartment, she feels a bit safer being herself. When she leaves, she feels pressure to put on makeup and eyelashes because feeling more stereotypically feminine helps her feel a little safer. CeCé feels pressure to have her hair down, her nails done, her clothes tight, and her cleavage showing. She puts time into grooming. Otherwise, she thinks her chiseled jaw, low voice, and muscles could lead to her being misgendered. This all, of course, matters in sports as well as life because "when you look good, you feel good and when you feel good, you perform well, you execute well."

When CeCé was competing, she felt a sense of freedom. She could be a body expressing itself. She could do things not everybody can do. She made extremely difficult athletic feats look effortless. Those are sweet feelings amid being bullied and ostracized on social media and in person. When CeCé stepped on the track, there weren't categories. She was just running. She was training to become the best athlete she could be. For a fleeting moment, she felt free.

When she stepped off the track, though, the boxes of where she fit appeared. Other people fought over where to place her, where she fit in society and in sport. Sports gave her an escape from her mind and an escape from society's pressure to fit gender binaries.

At the peak of her college career, CeCé placed first for her Division II school at Nationals in the 400-meter hurdles. Going into the race, she knew she was the person to beat. She finally felt like a competitive elite athlete. All the competitors had worked hard to be there, including her, and CeCé felt she deserved to compete and have a shot at winning. She loved being on the podium. She felt like she was ready to conquer the world.

Although CeCé could compete as a trans woman in an NCAA event, she couldn't compete at the next level. World Athletics bans trans athletes who transitioned after puberty from competing. Shortly after her NCAA win, CeCé saw her name on a list of thirty women athletes named to appear at the Olympic trials. Leading up to the Olympic trials, there are several events hosted in what is called a qualification window. Runners enter these events in hopes of winning, placing high enough, or posting a time that will funnel them into the pool of runners who compete in the Olympic trials. CeCé was briefly one of those runners and for a moment, her dream was coming true. Everything she had been working for was coming into focus. She felt empowered.

A few hours later, her name was taken off the list because she wasn't eligible as a trans woman. USA Track & Field (a subsidiary of World Athletics) determined that she could not prove her eligibility. USA Track & Field's guidelines do not allow trans women to compete. It felt defeating, tragic, and totally out of her control.

Some folks who had supported CeCé along the way as a queer athlete stopped supporting her as a trans athlete. She knew folks wanted her to quit and give up. Beyond college, she didn't have a coach and couldn't find one. Being an elite athlete is not like sports in grade school, high school, or college. Suddenly, she didn't have teammates; she felt utterly alone. It felt like her childhood. She is getting herself to the track and running her own workouts. She keeps training, looking forward to the next season, wanting to compete again, but currently she is ineligible and there is no pathway for her to participate as a trans woman.

Looking back, CeCé says that she could have chosen to join a gang instead of sports to keep herself safe and mask her femininity. She could have chosen suicide or turned to drugs. She could have taken her mom up on her idea to live a double life to appease her family, where she was married to a woman and had children while being trans in secret.

By choosing to be authentic to herself, she lost her family. It feels hard and lonely. She wonders if she would have achieved more in her running career if she'd had the support of her family. "I just feel like I don't have anybody to dream that dream with me, and it's just made the journey so much harder because I'm alone in this world. I'm never going to go back to the people that shunned me. You had your chance, and you blew it."

CeCé remembers being a fifth grader running in Jamaica. The dream still lives inside her. "I don't want to go to the Olympics and represent my country inauthentically." She wants to run as CeCé—a woman, and an awe-inspiring athlete. "People are going to have to see us. They are going to have to embrace the fact that we exist and we're not going to stop existing."

The prevailing cultural narrative that trans athletes pose a threat to cis athletes is harmful to trans athletes. There is no evidence that they are dangerous or hostile to their cis teammates. The policies restricting trans athletes in the name of protecting cis athletes stem from the same sexist logic that created sex segregation in sports to begin with. They assume that cis women are weaker than cis men, that trans women have the same biological makeup as cis men, and that trans men have the same biological makeup as cis women, and so, trans men aren't worth worrying about when they compete in men's sports. Let's have a better conversation about safety in sports that leads to more safety in sports for everyone. When presented with an imagined trans athlete that is out to do harm, let's think of trans athletes like Avery, Ciara, Finley, Peter, Robyn, Phoenix, and CeCé instead. Sports organizations, schools, and policymakers moving toward a more inclusive landscape that supports them, too, is a step in the right direction.

4

How Do We Better Support All Girls' and Women's Sports?

Myth: *Trans Athletes Are Ruining Women's Sports*

CONSERVATIVE POLICYMAKERS (WHO ALMOST NEVER HAVE A track record of supporting women) and anti-trans spokespeople are saying we must stop trans athletes from competing to protect cis girls and women. The implication is that trans women are ruining women's sports, which is simply not the case.

One story constructed by anti-trans spokespeople is that trans athletes are ruining women's sport because they are taking from the few hard-fought resources allocated to women. In short, the theory goes, trans athletes are stealing from cis women (be it medals, scholarships, or spots on teams). This is not true. No trans woman or trans man athlete has ever won an Olympic medal. Further, no out trans athlete has ever been awarded an athletic scholarship (or a Name, Image, and

Likeness deal, for that matter). Only two trans women have ever won a national championship—one was Lia Thomas and the other was CeCé Telfer.

Lia Thomas is a strong swimmer, but she did not place number one in every event. Thomas, just like any other athlete, wins and loses. In the 2022 NCAA Swimming Championships, Riley Gaines tied with Thomas in the 200-yard freestyle final for fifth place. Four other women beat Gaines and Thomas in that event. Gaines spoke on national television that she was upset to have not received a trophy for fifth place. Beyond this, Thomas placed last in other events (such as the 100-yard freestyle). There was no discussion of Gaines's overall low standings in the other individual event she competed in—the 200-yard butterfly—where she finished thirteenth. The numbers cited to talk about Thomas are cherry-picked to show extremes instead of the reality that Thomas won only a single event during NCAA Championships throughout her career. Most high-level swimmers win at least fifteen Championship events. When looking at Thomas's performance in the 500-yard free event as an example, here's what we know: Pretransition, Lia was ten seconds behind the men's record. Post-transition, she is ten seconds behind the women's record. What this tells us is that Lia has consistently been a high-performing athlete, not that she became one only post-transition. And, Thomas played by the rules: She met every criteria laid out by the NCAA to be able to swim, criteria that had been in place for over a decade and under which many trans athletes have participated with no issues.

The myth that trans girls and women are ruining women's sports relies on the scarcity model which distracts us from looking at why there is scarcity in women's sports in the first place and keeps us from addressing the core issues. Restricting and banning trans athletes' participation is not actually benefiting cis girls and women. It is leading to more gender policing of all girls and women, and it is not promoting participation in the female category. Women who call to restrict the rights of trans people do so to elicit patriarchal protection and support, yet inequality reigns.

Why do cis people feel threatened by diminished discrimination against trans athletes? It is the same reason as, according to Heather McGhee, author of *The Sum of Us*, "white Americans, who have thirteen times the median wealth of Black Americans, feel threatened by diminished discrimination against Black people."[1] Our country was built on the zero-sum game of slavery:

> Yes, the zero-sum story of racial hierarchy was born along with the country, but it is an invention of the worst elements of our society: people who gained power through ruthless exploitation and kept it by sowing constant division. It has always optimally benefitted only a few while limiting the potential of the rest of us, and therefore the whole.[2]

Instead of building a nation on a mutually dependent web, we are told to cling to what we have and make sure others lose more, even if it means us losing too. "The motive was greed; cultivated hatred followed."[3]

The clinging that comes with the scarcity of the zero-sum model is evident in policies that claim to restrict trans athletes to support women, while the policies are causing us all to lose. Elite athletes live in a cutthroat, take-no-prisoners, zero-sum game mentality at the top. If I win, you lose, and if you lose, I win. Trans inclusion gets emotional for cis elite athletes because they have fought so hard for what they have. Yet might it be misguided to bring this elite competitive mentality to youth sport and recreational sport? We see cis athletes and trans athletes pitted against each other, so desperate for a tiny piece of pie, that we can lose sight of our deep beautiful interconnectivity and the long-term goals of sports. Can we imagine a world where we are so clear on what real winning is that when a trans athlete who trained hard and performed well wins a medal, we all win?

To suggest that sports remain stagnant is unrealistic and historically inaccurate. Sports got better when women started competing. Sports got better when a good policy like Title IX supported a huge influx of girls and women in competition. We must trust that sports will continue to get better as trans, nonbinary, and intersex athletes feel safer competing.

States that have more inclusive trans policies also tend to have higher participation of cis girls in sports. This matters in a time when sports participation is dropping. Research from the Aspen Institute suggests that between 2019 and 2022, team sports participation for kids aged six to seventeen in the United

States declined 6 percent. Puberty and our society's standard of beauty has a shrinking effect on young girls, and play and sports can be an interesting corrective, teaching girls that they are agents of their bodies, that their bodies are powerful, that they can be the subject not the object, that they can take up space literally and figuratively. Yet girls remain twice as likely as boys to quit sport by age fourteen.[4]

Anti-trans bills and laws attempt to regulate access to gendering-affirming medical care for trans folks, but more than just their bodily autonomy is in jeopardy. Also at risk is their ability to make decisions about their identity, families, futures, and lives. Now is the time for cis and trans women to come together and fight like hell to get our bodies back. Our fates are intertwined.

Those interested in supporting cis girls' participation in sports can do so by supporting trans girls' participation. Both cis and trans girls are underrepresented at all levels of sports. Cis girls and women can be allies to trans girls and women. Protecting women means protecting trans women, too. The way forward is being paved by those individuals, teams, and sports organizations committed to supporting all girls and women, which in turn supports all athletes.

Yes, cis girls and women need our support in sports. Banning and restricting the participation of trans girls and women is not the way. To achieve an optimally inclusive sports landscape, we (trans and cis people alike) must advocate for policies that allow athletes to compete as they are, at every level, in supportive environments.

How can we better support all girls and women in sports?

Sports have been male dominated since antiquity.[5] In ancient Greece, men competed in feats of strength to display their masculinity. In the first Olympics, in 1896, only men competed.[6] In more modern times, sports have been used to cultivate grit and self-control in boys and men.[7] Women's bodies were deemed frail, especially while menstruating, and the idea was promoted that overexertion could affect a woman's ability to reproduce, even through the 1980s.[8]

Although women have been active in sports for thousands of years, they lacked opportunities, recognition, resources, and access until recently.[9] For centuries, Western culture perpetuated the idea that women are weaker than men—an idea that is alive and well today. When Kathrine Switzer and Bobbi Gibb snuck into the Boston Marathon in 1967, promoters of the race stated that women were too weak to run 26.2 miles.[10] People have limited the physical movement of women in the name of protecting them since sports began.[11]

As women gained greater access to sports over time, there was an alternative path available: Rather than strictly segregating sports by sex, competitions could have been integrated, allowing athletes to compete in ways that made the most sense across physical attributes. The sex segregation of sports was not inevitable but the result of a deliberate decision. Even today, with mandates in athletics for gender equity, schools and sports organizations have the choice to offer either sex-segregated or integrated sports and have continuously opted for segregation.

This structural inequality has resulted in criteria for success that favors men. Katie Barnes, in their 2023 book *Fair Play*, provides a telling example from figure skating. In competitive skating, a quad jump (a leap in the air where the skater completes four revolutions before landing) is considered more difficult, and therefore more valuable, than a complex series of spins. This judgment favors the physical attributes typically associated with male bodies, particularly in generating more height in jumps.

Since more male skaters successfully complete quad jumps, this leads to the perception that men are inherently more athletic. But, as Barnes points out, what if it didn't have to be this way? Imagine a world where a quad jump and a difficult sequence of intricate spins were valued equally, each seen as demanding in its own right. Here, a skater with exceptional spinning ability could compete against one with powerful jumps—not on the same moves, but on the merits of their respective strengths. Instead, the system favors jumping. That judgment may be less about difficulty and more about ingrained biases regarding what we consider superior "athleticism."

This example highlights the broader issue of how sports systems, and the values they uphold, are shaped by gendered assumptions. By privileging certain physical abilities, the system reinforces traditional notions of male superiority in athletics even when those abilities are not necessarily more difficult to achieve. This bias influences how we define athleticism and continues to disadvantage athletes whose strengths fall outside those predefined boundaries.

In their book *Open Play*, which calls for desegregating sports,

Sheree Bekker and Stephen Mumford argue that the differences in men and women in sports are created, not natural. Creating and maintaining women's sports as a category, then, deepens the subordination of women by assuming women cannot beat men. Women competing in sports is a radical and political act, and women's sports remains a patriarchal tool. Our sex-segregated sports system deepens the misconception that women's bodies are inferior instead of exploring how physical differences are manufactured and constructed. Misogyny and the patriarchy shape the roles and behaviors of girls and women over time. Instead of two categories of sports, where the former is the norm, designed by men for men (e.g., "the real sports"), and the latter for women as the inferior other, Bekker and Mumford call for a shift to feminist sports, which is for everyone and actively challenges the patriarchy. This would mean creating safe, protected spaces instead of segregated spaces. Feminist sports can help debunk the myths around women's bodies being fragile. It could help dismantle the patriarchy so we could see what liberated women are truly capable of.

There are people, teams, leagues, and organizations that have a prophetic imagination, that embody queer futurity, that insist on the potential of a different world, that can see a new way and are asking for a paradigm shift. Instead of fighting one another for scraps like we have been conditioned to do, all people can join cis and trans women to work together to challenge the assumptions and policies that limit us all.

*   *   *

Trans athletes are leading the way. Starlet, a trans woman golfer, loves engaging with folks different from her. One of her friends is a Catholic Republican who owns two guns. They respect each other as competitors and friends. She is patient with folks who have never heard her experience. So often in the media, there is no sound information presented; "If someone says something that is totally wrong, but they say it enough, people believe it."

Starlet tells people what they should and shouldn't say. She reminds them that just because she is sharing doesn't mean the next trans person is going to be in the mood to list every procedure they have had. With the support of her team and fans behind her, she is willing to go straight to the haters and humanize the issue of trans athletes in competition. "I've gone up to people after it and said, 'Do you want to have a beer and talk about it?' And they say, 'What do you mean?' I reply, 'Well, you said some shit. I'll sit down and you can say it to my face. We'll have a beer, we'll talk it out, and you can learn.'"

Similarly, Avery, a trans woman recreational softball player, is willing to engage in the opportunity to educate her cis teammates. When Avery does get to the bar after the game, they're brilliant. "Two guys from the ball team were talking about their friends who went to Thailand and were hanging out with lady boys, and I said, 'Well, you know the actual name is kathoey,' and they both looked at me like, 'What the fuck did you just say? How do you know that?' And I said, 'Come on, guys.'" And they all laughed together. Avery uses humor to defuse tense moments in a strategic way, bringing people along with kindness. They have a special positioning to speak up and address microaggressions with their voice and body. They say, "I actually think women and girls need more opportunities in sport and it really frustrates the hell out of me that there aren't enough opportunities for women but at the same time, not at a trans female's exclusion."

The fairness argument does not hold up in Avery's mind. They cite funding as an example and ponder if we'd ever create categories of athletes informed by a country's GDP or a family's wealth index. They look at the male athletes with sexual assault charges and wonder why they, as a trans woman, are the one being accused of being a predator. They write to organizations and the organization's sponsors, calling out their commitment to inclusion and pointing out the hypocrisy of their policies policing trans bodies.

"I feel that once I can talk to somebody, I can probably change their mind."

Cis folks can follow Starlet and Avery's modeling toward advocacy at the individual level. And we need more than individuals to shift gender equity in sports. There are small, local grassroots leagues leading the way. RecLeaguer is an organization that believes in sport for everyone.[12] Any adult who wants to play recreationally can sign up for a game, tournament, or league in several different sports and the organization will help you find a team, regardless of your experience or skill level. Their goal is to balance teams and make it easy for as many adults as possible to join and have a supportive community in which to move and play. A team does not have a set number of men or women or rules for how many women need to participate. Folks of all genders, sexes, and abilities say how healing and fun it is to come and play without category and have it feel appropriately competitive and fun (RecLeaguer, n.d.).

Athletes Unlimited is another example of a women's professional sports league with inclusive policies that include trans and nonbinary athletes. The organization recognizes gender beyond the binary and has a policy that creates a pathway to participation for trans and nonbinary athletes. Athletes Unlimited requires trans women and nonbinary athletes who went through puberty to suppress their testosterone in order to compete on the women's team. It seems to be working well. There are several other examples that show sports organizations creating new ways for all youths and adults to access the lifesaving power of sport.

Organizations like RecLeaguer and Athletes Unlimited are effectively responding to an overwhelming number of women's rights organizations which state that laws and policies targeting trans people harm all women and girls.[13] Scholars and women's organizations, including the Women's Sports Foundation, have conducted extensive research into the ongoing issues confronting women and girls in sports.[14] Compared with men and boys in sports, women and girls receive unequal opportunities, inequitable funding, fewer sponsorship opportunities, incomplete implementation of gender-equality policy in sports, uneven media coverage driven by gender stereotypes, and experience higher rates of sexual harassment and abuse.

These are the threats to women's sports that deserve attention. People working for women and girls are asking questions such as the following:

- Why do so few institutions in this country comply with Title IX?
- Why is media representation for girls and women severely lacking?
- Why did only recently the gold medal–winning U.S. Women's National Soccer Team achieve equal pay with the men's team?
- Why do Black and brown girls have less access to resources and drop out of sports at double the rate of their white, wealthy, suburban counterparts?
- Why is violence against girls and women so high in sports?

What you might notice is absent on this list of questions is a concern about trans athletes, and trans women in particular.[15] Systemic change focused on supporting trans athletes helps cis women rather than harms them. The Center for American Progress, for example, put out a study showing that states with trans-inclusive policies tend to have higher participation in girls' sports.[16] Narrow attempts to frame trans athletes as *the* problem for the survival of women's sports divert attention from far more pressing problems. Politicians bringing anti-trans bills to legislative tables do not have a history of supporting girls and women in ways that address these concerns.[17]

Policies that affect trans women's participation in elite sports are the continuation of a long history of exclusion of women from competitive sports—an exclusion that resulted in the introduction of a women's category in sports in the first place. The fact that sex regulation occurs only in the female category shows that the regulations are intrinsically discriminatory against women. Regulating trans women means regulating cis women.

For example, Annet Negesa, a middle-distance runner from Uganda, was tested to prove she was a woman with urine and blood tests. She was told she could not run in the 2012 Olympic Games and had to go to France for more testing. In Nice, she was told to return to Kampala to undergo a simple procedure. The procedure turned out to be the removal of internal testes. She had a painful recovery, lost her scholarship, and was left by her manager.[18] Women like Negesa from the Global South are disproportionately affected by pressure to undergo invasive and often unnecessary procedures to compete in the female category.[19]

Florida has proposed period tracking in schools to indicate gender. Several states that have introduced anti-trans legislation propose that eligibility for participation in the women and girls' category should be determined via invasive physical exams.[20] Legislators have suggested monitoring the testosterone levels of girls and women, testing their chromosomes, and inspecting their anatomy. Such proposals stem from contested policy changes at the international level that target gender-diverse women competing in elite sports.[21] Both the United

Nations and Human Rights Watch argue that such practices violate basic human rights and have lasting negative impacts on athletes, especially Black and brown women from the Global South, and athletes with intersex variations.[22] The proposed legislation could extend these eligibility requirements to cis athletes.[23]

Narrow definitions of how women should look harm cis girls and women. Suspicion-based testing provoked by superficial comparisons of the physical appearances of girls is capricious, and it disparages people who do not match stereotypical views of femininity.

Not only do cis girls and women face increased scrutiny from restrictions and bans on trans girls and women in sports, but they also miss out on the many benefits from having trans girls and women as teammates. Ally is a trans woman who, because she was raised as a boy, can now take on a role as an experienced mentor in a sport that has been historically male dominated.

Ally grew up in a small football town south of Grand Rapids, Michigan. She started football when she was seven and was good at it, enjoyed it, and rose through the ranks quickly. The physicality of the game hooked her. She loved having an arena set up to knock people around without hurting them. Tall and gangly, Ally played offensive line and linebacker. She was a student of the game, always gaining knowledge to fill in for her athletic vulnerabilities. In football, eleven athletes play offense and eleven play defense. When teams are small, athletes will play an offensive position and a defensive position.

Ideally, the team has enough athletes that they can specialize and get good at either offense or defense. By high school, Ally's team had enough athletes to specialize. Ally played defense as a linebacker, where she could run, fill gaps, and try to stop the offense from completing successful passes. She had a starting position on the highest-profile team in town. She found her place in the world. There was a sense of safety.

In small-town Michigan in the 1970s, there was no awareness around being trans. Ally knew she liked hanging around girls. She wished she were a girl, but that is where it ended. There was nowhere to put that energy. No one to talk to about it. Over the years, Ally explains feeling like a Jill-in-the-box. Life would grind away at her and every now and again the box would pop open, and Jill would come out. She'd want to put makeup on with her girlfriends in high school. As an adult, she'd want to hang out in the kitchen with the women while the men stood around the grill. She'd quickly slam Jill back in and close the lid because she didn't fit in the world around her.

Ally had a coach named Carl, who changed her life. He ran a group home for folks with severe mental illnesses. He was a dancer who would go into schools and invite students to move like primordial sea creatures as an improvisational dance. He was also an all-state quarterback with state championships as a player and as a coach. "I never once saw that man yell at anyone or even speak badly to anybody. He just knew that everybody was doing their best, but he also knew how to correct you if you were making mistakes." No other coach lived up to the standard that Carl set, and he remains the type of coach Ally aspires to be. "The coaches need to be examples of people, male or female, who can lead with love and include everybody."

When Ally was thirty-five, she saw a flier for a semipro men's football team. She stole a helmet from the youth team she was coaching and tried it on. It fit. She thought, "I think I can do this." She made the team, and they were the state champs for the next three years. She coached and played in the league for a decade.

Finally, in her fifties, Ally got sick of slamming the door shut on Jill. She decided to leave the lid open for a bit and see what happened. She experimented with gender expression[24] and took testosterone blockers and herbal estrogen, then pharmaceutical testosterone blockers and estrogen. "Literally, every step I took down that road felt one-hundred-percent right."

It took a few years for Ally to come out to herself and then to her family and her community. She had surgery to align her body, but it became clear she had to leave her community.

Ally had been married to a straight cis woman for thirty years when she began her transition in her early fifties. Most of her adult life she had been married to Sarah. She tried everything she could to be a good man and a good husband, but she couldn't make it work. They never found a way. It took a few years, but the marriage unraveled. She faced constant rejection, not as a person but as a lover, from the person she loved and adored. Sarah was supportive of Ally's transition but struggled with intimacy. They both decided it was time to part.

Ally moved from Maine to Los Angeles to start fresh. During that season of deep loss and grief, Ally discovered women's football and started playing. She explained, "So, the game has always been there for me." It was the thing she got to bring with her through her transition. "Maybe the reason that I love the game so much is that I've gotten to experience it on both sides of the gender marker. When I transitioned, I gave up so many things. I get to bring this along with me and play a game that I've played my whole life."

The women's football league welcomes trans women and Ally has always felt accepted by her team, though not by her opponents. Once, after a huge block, her opponent yelled, "We need a cup check on this bitch." But for the most part, she has been accepted. She contributed right away and found her home on a team and in the game that was a part of her. "That felt lovely." Now, at age fifty-nine, she is still going strong in a competitive national women's football league.

More than coaches or mentors, Ally talks about the game itself being her teacher. She lives for the camaraderie. She sees the person across from her as a necessary adversary and the other team as a necessary opponent. The game itself offers a stage for life to play out on. It has been a lifelong love. Looking her sixtieth birthday in the face and healing from a separated shoulder, she says, "I'm just not done." Her partner wishes she would pick a sport that wasn't so high-impact but the game continues to be a place she wants to be. Everyone has a role to play. "The game itself has never really let me down. Individuals, coaches let me down, players let me down, opponents let me down, but the game itself always seems to hold hope and challenge."

The game taught Ally perseverance, the need to prepare your mind and body, and the need to adjust in the moment. Things are never going to go as you plan them to go. "That is an acquired skill, that sort of calming your chaos is what I call it. People like me because I'm calm in almost all situations. Even when I'm angry, I tend not to go there much just because I know it's not really very productive, almost never really productive."

Moments of transcendence keep her coming back. Before a recent game, she had watched footage of the opposing team to prepare. She knew the other coach, and she knew her opponents. On a fourth down with one yard to go, Ally knew the opposing team was going to attempt a quarterback sneak. She timed it, blitzed through, and tackled the quarterback well behind the line of scrimmage for a huge loss, forcing a turnover of possession. She came off and apologized to her coach for usurping his play, and he said, "Ally, just play. Just do what you do."

To give you an idea of what a competitor Ally is, in the first game of a recent season she blew out her Achilles tendon. It didn't require surgery, but it was a nasty partial tear. Many people would take six months in a cast to heal from such an injury. Ally learned how to tape her own ankle, and midway through the same season, she was back on the field. In a pivotal moment of the game, she sprinted fifteen yards down the field, cut toward the center of the field to catch the toss, and scored a touchdown to win the game and ensure her team's entry into the playoffs. She lives for moments like this, but also for moments of teaching. She loves when great female athletes

walk onto her team with a love for sports but not much experience in football. Ally has the advantage of having decades
of football experience in her body. She loves passing on her
knowledge as a lifelong student of the game. People find their
way to football because it is a place you can work out your
aggression. You can hit other people for sport. She is a coach
who gets the physicality of the game and encourages others
to unleash their desire to have a safe outlet to run into other
people. Ally considers it a form of intimacy when it's done well,
with care and respect.

Whether she is coaching a team or playing on a team, football has always been a part of her life. "I can't seem to shake it,
no matter what I do." Three years after her gender-affirming
surgeries, her body is aligned with who she is. After a fast,
compressed puberty, where her body changed drastically and
quickly, she is beginning to declutter her wardrobe and claim
her body anew. With a refreshed relationship with her body,
Ally started acting and modeling.

Two years into her acting and modeling career, Ally landed
a role in a film with Brad Pitt in a fully nude sex dungeon
scene. It was another moment of arrival on the journey of coming out as trans. "To get booked as a fully nude woman in a
major Hollywood movie, it was amazing. It was like, 'Oh, well,
I know who I am but now they're recognizing who I am too, to
the point where out of thousands of people, I get cast.'"

After considering a facial feminization surgery, Ally recon-
sidered. "My insurance wouldn't cover it and since then, I've
kind of like come to terms with it. I don't really feel like I have

as much dysphoria about it as I used to, and I feel beautiful, and my partner thinks I'm beautiful. My cats don't care."

Ally's body has been through a lot. In addition to gender-affirming surgery, football has patterned itself in her joints. The right side of Ally's body—shoulder, hip, and knee—is rebuilt. Looking back, she sees part of her toughness stems from her childhood. She got love from her mom, who was low-drama, mature, responsible, and put together. Ally is softening around her perfectionism. Her injuries have taught her it is okay to take time to rehab and heal. She marvels at her ability to overcome adversity, reflecting, "I am amazed at what the human body can do." She wants to play as long as she feels like she is genuinely contributing.

Ally identifies with women warrior characters and wonders if she died in battle in a former life. Now an actor and model, she hopes to play a Viking leader. On the football field at age fifty-nine, she plays the role of wise warrior queen. "I don't want to be a legend. I want to play, and I want to teach others how to play, and I do it for love."

The love of battle lives in Ally's body. In a recent game, Ally lined up opposite her equal. They battled all game long. Her opponent's job was to block Ally all day, and Ally's job was to get through. Ally broke through a few times, but mostly it was an intense stalemate. The team photographer captured a moment of battle between these two women. She reflected, "There's poetry in it, there's music in it. There's physicality in it. It is just the joy of battle. We don't get to do it in our lives anymore. We're not warriors, and thankfully."

We often assume that anger, fear, shame, and violence are baked into football. Ally doesn't buy it. Ally is going to knock you down, but she is also going to help you up.

It is telling that the women's national football league welcomes trans women to play. In a game with a reputation for being a dangerous contact sport, cis and trans women in the league are disproving the assumption that cis women need to be protected from trans women.

Many of the organizations that have long championed women's rights have spoken out against policies to exclude trans women from sports.[25] The American Association of University Women, the Women's Sports Foundation, and the National Organization for Women, among others, argue that these exclusionary practices do more harm than good. These groups point out that banning trans women from sports only reinforces harmful stereotypes and undermines the progress made in athletics.[26]

High-profile women athletes like Megan Rapinoe, Candace Parker, and Billie Jean King have voiced their support for trans inclusion in sports. They, with nearly one thousand athletes and advocacy organizations, have made it clear through their advocacy in amicus briefs, legislative testimony, op-eds, and public posts that trans women belong on the field, court, and track alongside their cis peers. As Billie Jean King has stated, "There is no place in any sport for discrimination of any kind. The global athletic community grows stronger when we welcome and champion all athletes—including LGBTQI+ athletes."[27]

The bottom line is, participating in sports is about more than just winning. It's about teamwork, discipline, and personal growth. It's about breaking down barriers and creating spaces where everyone, regardless of gender, can thrive. This has been understood by powerful women in sports for decades. Trans women and girls deserve the same opportunities to experience the benefits of sports as their cis counterparts have. Excluding them not only harms them but also undermines the values of fairness and equality that sports are supposed to uphold.

Part of the magic of sports is that it puts people into close proximity. Having cis and trans athletes compete with and against each other in sports is an opportunity to build more compassionate communities. Em is a trans girl whose story shows how both she and her teammates benefit from her participation.

Before kids know how to tell other people that they are trans, many just live with a vague sense of difference. Em was an emotional child, and she felt pressure to suppress her emotions and be stoic in part because she was assigned male at birth. It didn't go well. Her peers made fun of her for being feminine, and she felt othered. Boys in her class seemed to have an easier time being detached and unemotional.

Sports, then, became a place to rest from the pressure and just play. Em played T-ball at age five and eventually baseball. She loved playing in the yard with her grandpa and her dad, and then loved the feeling of being on a team and sharing a common goal. There was nothing quite like when she or a teammate hit a long ball and the whole team erupted in cheers. "Well, it's very much being able to play with a team who accepts you. Everyone is just there to play, be together, work together."

At the beginning of the pandemic, Em was fourteen and starting the ninth grade. She had a lot of time to herself away from school and sports, and she began to differentiate from boys. "I really started feeling like I wasn't like everyone else, like something felt different, and it just took time for me to realize what it was. At first it was just kind of a feeling of not being comfortable in my own skin."

When Em heard coming out stories, they resonated with her. They felt familiar. During her year of at-home distance learning, she came out as a trans girl to her parents. Later that year, she came out to her wider community. When she and her fellow students returned to the school building, she had transitioned and started playing on the school volleyball and softball teams. She entered her high school for the first time as a sophomore, so many people did not need to unlearn her deadname and pronouns.[28] Others, who knew her before high school, took time to adjust.

Showing up to the girls' volleyball tryouts the August before sophomore year started was scary. "I was freaked out. I was super anxious and afraid of what might happen, especially because I'm not like all the other girls in a sense. You've done so much as this other gender and identity that trying to switch over and kind of fit in with that is really nerve-racking because you don't know what someone's going to say."

Luckily, it went well. Em's coach was supportive and

attentive, and when one teammate misgendered her and said unkind things about her behind her back, two of her teammates and her coach stepped in, stood up for her, and shut it down. Em found out about it all after the fact. It brought the team closer and built her trust in them. "I really enjoyed the team. They really had my back, and I made quite a few friends. It was really nice to be able to go to practice and have that feeling of safety and togetherness with everyone."

Being on a team helps Em to be brave. She feels like it is good to be different, and all the players can bring those differences together to work toward a common goal. In volleyball, you need strong bumpers, setters, and hitters, which requires different strengths and body types. In softball, you need strong infielders and outfielders. Pitching and catching are totally different skill sets. On most sports teams, diversity is a strength that is welcome and celebrated.

Baseball and softball have similarities, but they also have differences. Softball has a culture of being verbal, with lots of cheering. Em loved it. Her high school softball team combined with another school's because participation numbers were low, but the strong team dynamics were still present. Her teammates love her, in part, because she is so dedicated and team focused. She will do what it takes to improve and contribute.

Asked how it feels to play, she said, "Like you're not weighed down by anything else we have to deal with. It's this free-roaming area where you're able to just go out and play and enjoy everything to your heart's content. You feel really light and able to move." Playing sports on a girls' team as a trans girl, according to Em, "Just felt right, like being able to truly feel like I fit in with everything and being able to know that it's okay that I'm different from others." On her teams, it was a collective competitive advantage to having diversity of body types. It was good to be different together, finding the right position and role for your particular strengths and working toward a common goal.

Em believes sports can be a space free of restrictive gender rules:

> Because to me, that has nothing to do with why you play a sport. I have a friend who is cis female, and she plays football. And she has similar experiences where the guys kind of mistreat her or push her around because she's female, so she's not going to be as good as them, and then she shows them up for it. She puts in twice as much, three times as much work as the rest of them do because she shows that she's supposed to be there and that she has the talent and ability to play at the same level as them.

Em is the first openly trans athlete to compete for her school. To prepare to participate on the girls' teams, she put in weeks of filling out forms, getting letters of recommendations, getting doctors' and therapists' notes, and compiling name-change and gender-change information for her state high school league. Em has the approval of her coaches and athletic director to compete in girls' softball and volleyball.

Having official approval from the state high school league too means that no school she plays against can oppose her participation and accuse her team of cheating. Each state is different. Some say youth athletes must compete in the category they are assigned at birth or not at all.

In 2019, twenty of the fifty United States offered policies which ensured trans students under the age of eighteen could participate in sports on a team based on their gender identity, seventeen had policies that prohibited participation, and thirteen had no standard policy.[29] By 2024, twenty states have banned trans youth (and in most cases, adult) athletes from participating in sports consistent with their gender identity.[30] This landscape is made even more complicated by laws that apply in school but not in sports played outside of school.

For example, twenty states have laws that prohibit discrimination in schools on the basis of sexual orientation and gender identity.[31] However, living in a state without a ban on sports participation based on gender identity does not mean athletes cannot be denied opportunities to try out for a team. For instance, in 2024, two of those twenty states (Iowa and Virginia) had laws that prohibited discrimination in schools based on gender identity and laws that banned trans athletes.[32]

Of the sixteen states that have a friendly or inclusive policy at the state level, two states (Florida and South Carolina) have laws banning trans youths from playing sports, which supersede existing high school policies.[33] After a state high school athlete association creates a trans inclusive policy, state lawmakers can come in after and overshadow it. These dichotomies highlight the complexity and the confusing nature of the athletics policy landscape for trans athletes across the United States.[34]

In Em's state, it is up to her coaches, administrators, and high school leagues if and where she will compete. Coaches and administrators, who are not often educated on trans identities, are getting educated so that they can make informed decisions that support the well-being of youth athletes. For youths, before or during puberty, requirements that adult trans women athletes are subject to, such as having to undergo gender-affirming hormone treatment before competing in the female category, can feel more fraught. There is no good research to inform these policies as they apply to youths.

Em thinks it is worth it to pave the way for other trans and nonbinary kids who want to play sports. Her trans and nonbinary friends tend to stick to what she calls academic sports, like robotics or quiz bowl, because trying out for teams as a trans kid brings "judgment on when you go to play, especially depending on if you've done meds or surgeries or any of that starting off. Going in, very much looking like a cis man or woman, and playing your identified gender sport, it brings a lot of controversy with it, and a lot of people use it as a way to get to you because you're different."

Playing volleyball as a trans girl was different from softball. Maybe because of the attire, that the uniform is more fitted and there is no helmet like in softball, Em did not always fit the physical stereotype of a girl volleyball player. At certain away games, Em noticed more security present, more monitoring of the student section, anticipating friction. The hate pushed Em.

"A lot of it just turned into me working even harder to show that you want to say that it's wrong for me to be here. I'm going to prove to you why it's right and why I've earned my spot here." Early on in Em's high school sports career, opposing teams and cheering sections got vocal. Each time, Em's advocates sent emails to the principals and athletic directors of those opposing schools in such a high volume that when she returned to those schools, the team would always break out a few more rainbows and trans flags in support of Em.

How Em's parents, coaches, and teammates are showing up for her speaks volumes. They have her back, which is what being on a team is all about. They are carving out space for Em to play freely and thrive. The pressure they put on principals and athletic directors, the people who have the power to change school policy and influence culture, worked. It made Em's sports competitions safer, more inclusive, and a more positive place for everyone. The youth athletes on Em's team and on the opposing teams are learning and growing. Every trans youth athlete deserves that kind of advocacy and support.

Now that Em is a senior, her hard work has told the truth. At first, when Em was on a junior varsity volleyball team with no experience, jealous teammates said it was because she "used to be a guy." Em showed up day in and day out, trained hard, and dedicated herself to the team and the game, proving that both physicality and hard work are necessary for success. "I put the work in to be where I want. I spend time every practice every day getting ready, practicing what I need to, making sure that

I've worked on my abilities to the best I can to go and play." She worked to prove that she belonged:

> I probably had to work three to four times harder than everyone else. I would take extra time if the coach offered it, spend extra time working on the drills and how to run certain plays or memorizing how the positions work. And doing my absolute best to catch up kind of to where everyone else was and show that I got put there because they saw that I had the potential to be there and that I was willing to put the work in to be there.

In addition to supportive teammates and coaches, Em's mom is an advocate. "Mom is very much the first one to push and fight back against what she thinks is wrong, and she will very much bend the rules to show what needs to be done and what needs to be said. She's also not against going straight above the heads of others to get to a different level that has power to help change things and make things better."

Em's mom gives her the courage to keep going. She has worked hard just to be able to play:

> I'm only there to play the sport and be a part of the team. I wish they knew how hard it was to try and fit in and be a part of that community. How it takes so much more effort and so much more strength to

show up every day and be a part of the same things that a lot of people take for granted when they do a sport. Being able to walk out onto the court, the field, and showing you belong and that it's okay to be there.

It is joy that keeps Em coming back to sport. "I think one of the biggest things that gives me joy is being able to walk onto the court or field of my chosen sports and knowing I worked my hardest to be there, I worked my way to where I am, and that I'm playing with a team and with coaches who accept that and are ready to play me and have me be a part of the team like anyone else."

Why would anyone want to restrict that?

When we talk about transgender athletes in youth sports, we have to continually remind ourselves that we are talking about kids. Their brains are not fully developed, nor are their bodies. They need adults and systems to support them, advocate for them, and carve out safe spaces for them to learn and grow. In an ideal world, play is a child's full-time job, no exceptions.

In listening to Em's story, it is striking and moving that she has a network of adults who are supporting her so that she can be a thriving child who knows how it feels to play unencumbered. What if all kids felt that way?

The myth is that trans athletes are coming in droves to steal medals and do harm. This narrative is fear based and it is creating a culture of scarcity. Scarcity is already alive and well in women's sports because sports have been so inequitable for so long. Advocates in Em's story are taking on an abundance mindset to talk back to these scarcity-producing myths. How can more of us follow their lead and, instead of putting energy toward banning and restricting trans athletes, put that energy toward supporting all girls and women in sports?

Because sport has been shaped around the cis male body, however, our bias deepens. The rules prove our hunch. Women are compared with men and deemed inferior, when in reality, there is both bias and physiology at play. Sports were created by men for men, prioritizing power and strength. Women are deemed less athletic because they are playing catch up in a game rigged for them to lose.[35]

We have limited research on bodies that are not cis and male. Between 2014 and 2020, 6 percent of sports science research focused exclusively on women, and women made up only 34 percent of research participants.[36] Menstruation, sports bras, and eating disorders (which impact men too) are underexamined.[37] This vacuum of research has an impact on cis women and trans, intersex, and gender expansive folks in all aspects of sports including equipment, activewear, protective gear, injury prevention, recovery, and strategic training plans.[38]

To combat the head start that men got in shaping sports, women have fought hard to be disobedient of the signs and to make some new ones, creating policies that gave women a better chance to participate. Title IX is a landmark federal civil rights law prohibiting sex-based discrimination at any school or educational program that received federal funding.[39] After its enactment, the number of girls and women participating in sports exploded.[40] In that time, there was conversation about whether we should continue with sex-segregated sports or shift to support girls and women participating with boys and men. Now, it is hard to imagine a sports system that is not sex segregated. Title IX allows, but does not require, sex segregation in sports and focuses on issues related to equal resources and opportunities.

Since Title IX's passage, women's participation at the high school level has grown by 1,057 percent and by 614 percent at the college level.[41] The Paris Olympics in the summer of 2024 was the first since 1896 that 50 percent of Olympic participants were women.[42]

Today, over fifty years after Title IX was passed, women are still underrepresented in sports, leadership, and media. Women athletes and their sports programs still have fewer teams, fewer scholarships, and lower budgets than their male counterparts.[43] Recent data shows that NCAA women's sports programs received only half as much financial support as men's, including 46 percent as much on recruiting and 43 percent on coach compensation.[44]

In team sports, 7 percent more men than women play, and there is a 22 percent gap between girls and boys.[45] Girls have 1.3 million fewer opportunities to play high school sports than boys have.[46] We also see clear gender gaps when we look at the number of women working in sports at every level.[47] Women are in the minority in coaching and other leadership positions—and numbers have dwindled even further since the enactment of Title IX.[48] Sexual harassment and abuse against women athletes runs rampant.[49] Huge pay gaps remain: Spotrac reported the highest NBA salary at \$51,915,615, while the highest WNBA salary falls at \$234,936.[50] There is a long-standing record of work being done to expand access to women's sports.[51] But there is still ample work to be done.

Less than 2 percent of all sports media coverage is of women (except during the Women's World Cup and the Olympics, when those numbers sometimes spike to about 4 percent).[52] Meanwhile, less than 0.05 percent of all sports coverage is of trans men and nonbinary athletes.[53] Generally, anyone who is perceived to have a woman's body is considered irrelevant in sport.[54] This irrelevance—what it looks like in the everyday—tells us a lot about how sports operate and about our culture.

We are seeing women's sports bars like the Sports Bra in Portland and A Bar of Their Own in Minneapolis pop up and thrive. They are dedicated to showing only women's sports, pointing not only to the discrepancy in media coverage but also to the growing support of women's sports.

The benefits of Title IX are many.[55] But debates abound about Title IX and trans inclusion in sports persist. Should Title IX be used to support the inclusion or exclusion of trans athletes? Folks are citing Title IX on all sides of the conversation. And as Title IX has become a focal point in the debate over trans athlete participation, contrasting views have emerged around how it should be interpreted.

As many of us know, LGBTQ people's mental health is

disproportionately affected in sports, and still, data, research, and best practices are not well known. Because coaches' knowledge about LGBTQ language and topics correlates with support for trans athletes, a foremost priority is to equip those who work directly with athletes with language and knowledge of LGBTQ topics. Transathlete.com and Athlete Ally are two great places for coaches to go to equip themselves to be advocates.[56]

More than 32 percent of NCAA institutions are Title IX exempt or are in states with anti-LGBTQ sports or medical care laws that affect NCAA athletes.[57] In turn, nearly a third of NCAA athletes can be actively discriminated against because of their sexual orientation or gender identity.[58] Helping athletes, athletics personnel, and institution administrators to become aware of these realities and working to mitigate these laws can serve to protect athletes.[59] What is more, cis athletes, coaches, and administrators are responsible for educating themselves so they can become more effective at their jobs and can advocate for all their athletes. It should not fall on trans athletes to do all the educating. Folks in power must take responsibility for knowing proper language, support, and protocols for their trans athletes.

One perspective, generally citing Title IX in anti-trans advocacy, argues that in the name of protecting women's sports, trans women athletes should be barred from competing in the female category.[60] Proponents of this view argue that allowing trans women in the women's category harms the limited space and power cis women currently have in sports.[61] They think that trans women should compete with cis men and want to keep the women's category limited to cis female bodies that fit their idea of femininity.[62] In March of 2024, a group of former college athletes filed a lawsuit against the NCAA, stating that allowing Lia Thomas to compete in the National Championship in 2022 had violated Title IX.[63] Under political pressure, the NCAA hastily scaled back its previous policy, which offered a path to inclusion for trans athletes receiving gender-affirming care. While the lawsuit is ongoing, the American Civil Liberties Union (ACLU) and the National Women's Law Center (NWLC) filed a motion to dismiss the case in May of 2024, citing severe flaws in legal and factual statements presented in the complaint. [64]

Others argue Title IX is meant to protect trans and non-binary folks because, while Title IX states that it protects *sex*, they interpret sex to mean one's *gender*. This interpretation of Title IX has been used in past lawsuits, not yet in sport, but in broader educational settings. For example, Gavin Grimm, a trans boy, won a landmark case in Virginia allowing him to use the boys' bathroom at school by leaning on Title IX. Collectively, people who use this interpretation of Title IX believe it cannot and should not apply only to cis women and, in turn, be used to discriminate against marginalized and underrepresented groups. At the end of the day, they contend, Title IX is about equal opportunities and ensuring all underrepresented people can play sports, so cis boys have successfully cited Title IX to play on girls' teams where there was no opportunity for boys.

One barrier is that we have severely limited research on the female body, as well as limited research on trans, nonbinary, and intersex bodies and how they relate to athleticism. As more trans, intersex, nonbinary, and gender expansive athletes are coming out and seeing no place to fit, we are realizing more fully how under-resourced we truly are in knowledge. What if we saw the work to support women in sports as the work to support all bodies that are considered less than? This is an opportunity to make sports better for everyone instead of fighting over leftover scraps.

Sports have historically confronted and challenged definitions of womanhood, and there have always been anxieties and tensions about who fits. Remember Caster Semenya, who we mentioned previously, and the lengths she had to go to compete in the women's category? Race plays a role here, too, as do intersex variations. We can perpetuate the policing of female and gender expansive bodies, or we can work to undo some of the flawed assumptions that hold the exclusion of certain bodies that do not fit society's limited idea of women.

We see the real threats to women's sports continue to be sexual abuse and harassment, unequal pay and resources, and a lack of women in leadership positions. These are documented threats and challenges to fairness and equality in women's sports that athletes have been talking about for decades. Folks who want to cite Title IX and the protection of women can make strides by coming together and working for sporting spaces that support all women—cis and trans alike—from discrimination so we can all be our true selves. Can we work together toward a sporting society where trans bodies get to flourish, too?

Plenty of people, teams, organizations, and leagues believe that trans inclusion is not a problem but the way forward toward safer and more enriching sporting environments for all athletes.

Certain sports and pockets of the sports world are ripe for being imaginative when it comes to trans inclusion. Recreational powerlifting is one such pocket. Recreational powerlifting leagues and gyms could drop gender categories without much fanfare because it is, like so many other sports, no contact. It is ultimately the lifter against themselves.

Competitions can be categorized by weight class without adding an overlay of gender. And there are people and gyms doing precisely that.[65] Hannah Wydeven owns a gym called Solcana in Minneapolis that makes a habit of questioning assumptions about segregation based on gender. Does it serve anyone to say that women use a 35-pound bar and men use a 45-pound bar? Who makes the weight classes and what assumptions inform them? What is the purpose of dividing people by sex?

After playing softball in college, Hannah worked at a gym as a trainer. Eventually, her boss fired her because she wanted to offer women-only classes. Unemployed, she decided to open her own gym. Solcana started out as a gym that was a safe space for women to feel seen. It quickly became a queer space, too. She knew she needed to do some homework about colonization and hormones so that her gym could also feel safe for trans folks and people of color. She hired and trained fat people, trans people, and people of color so that her leadership would represent the community.

CrossFit used to be a hard world for trans folks to feel safe so Hannah dropped the CrossFit affiliation at her gym and focused on powerlifting. Eventually, CrossFit's policies on trans participants reflected the International Olympic Committee language. CrossFit is now more inclusive than is powerlifting.

Over the years, a few of the trans powerlifters from Solcana wanted to compete. Hannah entered trans men into lifting competitions in the male category, and no one objected. The trans men competed without fanfare. When Hannah registered trans women for competitions in the female category, however, they were met with resistance. The double standard infuriates Hannah and the Solcana community and has led her to be an outspoken advocate for trans powerlifters.

Solcana continues to be a safe place for women, fat, queer, trans, and people of color to move and gain strength. The gym gives a glimpse of what is possible and shows that focusing on inclusion can benefit the whole community. Hannah's personal rules for being a cis ally are simple:

Believe trans people.

It is no one else's job to make me comfortable.

Question every rule and see how it is upholding the dominant culture.

Just because you haven't lived it doesn't mean it's not real.

You are not saving them. You are making room for them to

make your community better and providing tools for them to thrive.

Don't insert yourself unless you have been called on to do so. There is enough for everyone.

Also in Minneapolis, the Twin Cities Goodtime Softball League (TCGSL), now part of the North American Gay Amateur Athletic Alliance, started in 1979 with a game between the Minneapolis Police Department's softball team and the first openly gay softball team in the city, sponsored by a gay bar called the Saloon.[66] The game drew a gigantic crowd, and the Saloon team won, making headlines. G stood for goodtime because the G could not yet safely stand for gay.

Today, the TCGSL league has fifty-two teams with any combination of cis, trans, queer, and straight players.[67] The Twin Cities hosted the Gay Softball World Series in 2023. On any given night a team with trans folks may play a team of gay men or a team of all lesbians or a team of all cis men who are gay and straight. It transcends the gender binary. The players love the variety and makeup of the league. The teams feel like safe spaces for people to connect to play hard and have fun. It's a highlight of the players' week and a pillar of their embodied journey. TCGSL gives me hope that sports can be a space for healing and breaking down binaries that limit us as athletes and people.

Places intentionally creating queer- and gender-equitable sports spaces like RecLeaguer, Solcana, and TCGSL support cis athletes while mattering deeply to trans athletes navigating a very cis and binary sports landscape. Peter, a trans man and former lacrosse player, found a co-ed adult soccer team where he felt competitive and as though he could really contribute to the team. He doesn't get pushed off the ball like he used to. He also feels safe. "Nobody doubted my gender in any way. I was never misgendered, and it felt good to be good at something." Part of what made him feel safe on this team was that the members were diverse and gender inclusive. The ball was passed to him not because he was a guy but because everyone got passed to, regardless of gender. Peter also got into outdoor recreational activities, which felt therapeutically nongendered: "There's no, 'We're going to count how many guys and how many girls entered this park, and we're going to make sure that their ratio is correct.'"

Outdoor recreation has helped Peter see the strengths and advantages of his body and its journey:

> There are many things about my body that are impossible to change, and it's not a productive emotion for me to resent the fact that I didn't get the chance to truly go through the puberty that would give me the body that I feel like I should have. I've gotten into slacklining recently, and one thing that I try to tell myself is that the fact that I have a lower center of gravity than most cisgender men is an advantage to balance.

Similarly, Eli, a trans man who competes in skydiving, explains how the sport made it easeful for him to be trans. In competitive skydiving, there are no men's and women's divisions. Teams can be made up of any combination of humans, and the best team wins. Creating an all-women's team is an option, but at the national level, they don't compete separately. This creates a culture where nonbinary and trans athletes can feel welcome, included, and supported at all moments on their journey. Many sports scholars agree that the way competitive skydiving categorizes participation could be a good step for other sports to take.

While on the national skydiving team, Eli took up powerlifting to cross-train and strengthen his upper body. He felt powerful in his body being able to squat 300 pounds but the gym was gendered. The parking lot was filled with pickup trucks with bumper stickers supporting the firefighters and police force and American flag decals. The gym was filled with white guys who slapped you on the back of the neck and screamed at you to get you pumped up. It was also the kind of gym where guys called each other "pussy" and "faggot" as insults, also to pump each other up.

Eli used humor to defuse these situations and call the guys in, and it worked:

> Some of the guys would start, "Don't be such a p—"
> or "Stop being a f—" and then stop, look at me, and
> say, "Sorry, man." One day one of the guys said to

me, "You know, man, if someone had told me that one of my favorite people was going to be a tranny, I wouldn't have believed it." I said, "If somebody had told me one of my favorite people would be a Jehovah's fucking Witness, I wouldn't have believed it." We just had fun together. We both really dug each other. I like to think that maybe someday he's with a bunch of friends out in the country and maybe he corrects one of them on something or maybe there's someone they leave alone because he says, "Hey, guys, let's go do something else." I don't know. But that exposure is important. I think that's been something I've loved about a bunch of different sports I've done with a lot of these white people from the country is that I'm the first or one of the only trans people they know. That's really cool at some level.

Eli sees it as educational deprivation. He is willing to meet folks where they are and bring them along.

Ultimate frisbee is another arena creating a new. Ciara, one of the trans women runners we interviewed, also got into frisbee. She joined a women's team and is having a better experience. There is no toxic masculinity. The leaders are approachable. There is a community, cooperative feel. The ultimate field became a place for Ciara to practice life. "Playing a women's game now, especially in a beginner's league, the focus is entirely different, and I really love that. My ultimate nights are the highlight of my week."

She sees ultimate as a sport and recreational leagues as a level that can lead the way forward for trans inclusion. Running supported Ciara through her darkest days. Frisbee is infusing her life with community, meaning, and joy. Within sports, Ciara says, "I think it's a misconception to apply the Olympic model to all of sport. That ignores all the other equally important functions that sport plays in society. Fostering acceptance, and teaching teamwork, and independence, self-confidence. All those other great lessons that sport teaches in its unique way. I think yes, absolute performance is an important consideration, but it shouldn't drown out those other considerations."

There is no magic sport, however. It takes a league, a team, and players willing to work against misogyny toward gender equity and trans inclusion. Kenny found their people playing ultimate frisbee in college. On their first team at the University of Virginia, they beautifully articulated that "the queerness held you." There was a trans man on the team who acted like a beacon. Then in grad school, Kenny still had eligibility left and played for University of Colorado Boulder. That team joked that they had the same number of ACL tears as straight people. Kenny had a queer coach who saw them and challenged them to be more authentic to themself. The team became their main source of community, friendship, and belonging. They felt so safe, so free.

Kenny said they came out as trans out of both necessity and choice. It was a leap of faith, trusting their instinct, that there was something more authentic, more fulfilling, more real, and richer to be had. They chose to imagine a different way of being.

Kenny's team placed second at Nationals their last two years of grad school. They got off a plane from college Nationals and drove straight to a club ultimate tryout. On the mixed club team, Kenny did not feel the same sense of belonging. As a trans nonbinary athlete, Kenny continually questioned where they fit in.

USA Ultimate, the national governing body for ultimate frisbee, allows athletes to register into the category where they feel most comfortable. In college, there is a men's and a women's category. Kenny played on women's teams, saying the culture there was intentionally open and gender expansive. In club frisbee, there are mixed, women, and open divisions. The open division effectively acts like the men's division. Kenny could compete on any of the three. Kenny's club team was mixed. On mixed teams, binaries can sneak in because players match up against opponents to guard one-on-one. Some mixed teams, including Minneapolis's Drag'n Thrust, San Francisco's Polar Bears, New York's XIST, and Seattle's BFG, use nongendered language to match their players, like "Novas" and "Psions" instead of "men" and "women." But Kenny's club team didn't, and the team culture did not leave room for gender expansive folks. Kenny wondered whether he should match with an opposing man or woman:

> Every time my teammates and I counted my body toward the "woman matching" ratio on the line, my stomach knotted. Likewise, my outspoken demeanor grew tired; I put time and effort into conversations

with the team about gender and biology, hoping that a thoughtful, personal, and scientifically-based approach to these topics would solve my dysphoria in that space. Frequent misgendering incidents and gendered language made me increasingly on edge as the season marched along. My mind ran out of space for frisbee strategy and analysis; my motivation and enthusiasm similarly ebbed.

Kenny felt limited in how mixed ultimate still categorized into "woman" and "man." Ultimate changed the language to "woman matching" and "man matching," but the labels still felt binary to Kenny, who is wholeheartedly nonbinary:

Within a mixed space, we can practice seeing each person for who they are as a whole person, and yet we exist within and prop up a structure that makes it very easy to sort each player into one of two categories and to correspondingly hold them to different standards. Part of why mixed was so hard for me is that I was constantly trying to remind my teammates and my opponents, and at times myself, that I was not a woman and that my matchups were not "woman matching." We can change the language we use to count bodies, but we are still counting bodies.

Kenny trudged through that first club season, but as they

started gender-affirming hormone treatment and looked ahead to chest surgery, they wondered, "Can I keep playing?"

Their doctor replied, with calm reassurance, "This is the problem of your generation. No matter what you do, it will be wrong, but you should play your sport. I can't tell you what the right answer is, but you will know where you belong." Kenny didn't feel belonging on their club team, and they wanted that belonging back from when they started ultimate. So, they started their own team. "I waffled between 'making it work' on an existing team and leaving the sport for the time being. Neither option felt right in my body." But with some courage and imagination, there is a third way, even if we have to make it by walking it. Kenny and a friend decided to create a place to belong:

> Our team would compete in the women's division. Our team would be overwhelmingly queer. Our team would be a home for trans athletes. I wish to queer the existing space, to redefine the basis itself by staying and playing our sport. For now, we are to work within the confines of existing structures, but we will bend and expand and reimagine what those structures look like and how they operate, and when they become unrecognizable as compared to where we started, we'll know we've made a difference.

Colorado Kelp (Kind, Enthusiastic, Loving People), a club women's team, was born and is thriving. They believe community is their strength and that trust and love are competitive advantages. Women's teams don't have to retrofit gender inclusivity into a matching system. Colorado Kelp is made up of nonbinary, transmasculine, trans men, cis women, and gender expansive players. Everyone belongs, so they can drop into their bodies and play. Kenny plays better on this team because they feel safe and liberated, less skittish. They explain, "Playing on Colorado Kelp feels like coming inside after squinting outside on a summer day. When you come inside, your eyes can relax. You feel both relief and the fatigue of squinting for so long."

In their manifesto, Kenny writes,

> Trans participation in team sports is radical because we must work against a system that was not designed to include us. Trans participation in athletics shows us what is possible off the field, in other spaces and in our relationships. Trans participation is necessary if we are to call ourselves and our sport inclusive and fair. Our new team, Colorado Kelp, is born out of hope for a space that nurtures persons who want to play and laugh, sing and dance, and throw the frisbee and our bodies around. We can do those things, safely and comfortably, when we are in community with others who see us for who we are and believe in our right not only to exist but to be free. We deserve to play our sport. We deserve to belong in ultimate. We will sway in the currents, reach up to and bask

in the sun, and provide nourishment and refuge for
countless creatures. We will be a team and a community. We are a movement towards the more inclusive and expansive future that we envision today.

Kenny sees their role as pushing back on simple categories,
living in liminal spaces even when it feels exhausting and isolating, so that they can encourage others to live authentically
too. Colorado Kelp has been a balm, a community that is larger
than the sum of its parts. They are a group of athletes queering the structure so more bodies can exist and feel safe, while
requiring straight and cis players to commit to being vocal
advocates for their teammates. A new way is coming into being.

Journalists play a role too. Journalists have an opportunity to
tell a new version of the story and report on stories that are
trying inclusion instead of exclusion in sports. A distinct
few journalists, media pieces, and sports broadcasters trouble
assumptions about gender and sex segregation in sports in helpful ways. They present athletes as complex, with multiple identities, and show how trans athletes must navigate and negotiate
systems of oppression. Katie Barnes, for example, writes about
trans and nonbinary athletes in a way that challenges the status quo. In their cover story of Layshia Clarendon for ESPN
in 2021, Barnes describes how Clarendon, a nonbinary athlete
competing in the WNBA, used basketball to explore sexuality, identity, and justice. Barnes describes Clarendon as an athlete, parent, organizer, activist, and trailblazer and commends

them for influencing conversation in basketball on issues like LGBTQ rights and police brutality.[68]

If sports consumers and writers thought and wrote about gender differently, were critical of it as a construct and not an inevitable categorization, trans and nonbinary athletes could be welcomed into the fold. Sports got better when women were included. Sports got better when people of color were included. We imagine and believe sports will be better when trans folks are included. If we can discuss categorization more strategically, we can disrupt the rhetoric that assumes and reinforces the superiority of cis men. Journalists and writers have the opportunity to shift narratives about trans athletes in a way that allows trans athletes and cis female athletes to disrupt a rigid binary sex segregation in generative and helpful ways.

There is a lot of misinformation about trans women and girls in sports; there is not enough information about trans boys, trans men, intersex, gender expansive, and nonbinary athletes. Trans athletes play sports for the same reason cis athletes play—they love the game, they thrive on its mental and physical benefits, and they desire the community and camaraderie that can lead to a sense of belonging.

The focus on banning trans athletes has elevated to a high conflict in the United States. Folks who want to ban trans athletes from competing believe that they are moral and right, which is prioritized above being compassionate toward the experience of trans athletes. We are living in a moment of divided political radicalism, and trans folks are being restricted unfairly. Politicians have and are seeking more power and money than ever. Sports institutions have and are seeking more power and money than ever. Trans athletes are more vulnerable than ever. And there is a clear commitment toward maintaining and growing the gaps between those who have power and money and those who do not.

By not paying attention, we allow conservative policymakers to assert control over trans bodies. Health care is a human right and so is access to play. Whether your body is being restricted by policy or not, it is time to speak up and talk back to these policymakers who are privileging bodies that look like theirs to maintain their power and control.

Trans women and girls are being spotlighted and vilified in the media. The narratives of trans folks being the problem are adding to the anti-trans rhetoric and sentiment. Silence about the oppression of trans folks is deafening. We see media covering bans more than media covering violence done to trans people.

At this moment, cis people have the power to open doors for trans people to participate in sports at every level. U.S. politicians are making decisions that deny sports participation. The head of an exclusive golf club acts as a gatekeeper to play. Some kids on the playground decide which other kids can play. There are those who have an inevitable right to play, and others who do not. There are the free, the gatekeepers of sports, and the freed, those they decide to let in.

Bodies that are indisputably white, cis, and straight move up in the world. Living with those identities can slip us into underexplored, privileged bodies that perpetuate the status quo. Cisgender, gender expansive, intersex, nonbinary, and trans people can come together to build a world where sex cannot exploit us, a world where we are free of the tyranny of biology.

There will be consequences. Fear of losing relationships, jobs, and opportunities is real, but what we get instead, if we commit to the work over time, is our dignity, our exuberance, our joy, our self-respect, and our freedom. The media buzz about trans athletes is doing work. We froth and chum over critical race theory, gender-neutral bathrooms, banned books, the rights of fetuses, and the motives of Taylor Swift, while the rich get richer and those in power stay in power. Cis women worry about trans women hurting the female category instead of seeing how the structure hurts us all. We could come together pissed as hell to challenge cis men with millions of dollars who believe and write policies that look out for themselves. The work for better policy requires us all—but especially cis men and women—to explore our own bodies and our beliefs about our own bodies and to be willing to release our grip on a false sense of cis privilege in the name of joy.

Folks who support trans exclusion may do so because trans people are free in a way that few of us have recognized or explored. Trans freedom and trans joy are perceived as threats only if you have not recognized how our binary world limits us all. Maybe deep down, cis people are jealous of trans people because it seems that they are getting away with something. They are living the truth that gender is a dynamic performance that we learn and live and being obedient to the rigid world of cis-ness, in fact, limits humanity for the rest of us too.

James Baldwin might tell us that cisgender people who hate transgender people won't let go of their hate because then they would have to deal with their pain. Jane Ward asks if her straight friends are okay because the culture of heterosexuality can be untenable for women.

Similarly, cisgender women working to exclude transgender women from sport have endured the pain of fighting to build up the female category and the deep desire to be in feminine spaces that feel safe. If those of us who have body privilege and systemic power can turn toward the pain in our bodies and name what we lose in our constant obedience to the system, we can start doing the healing work necessary to get free.

Healing is hard, but so is not healing. Not healing requires suppression, repression, and denial. It requires holding on to anger and hatred. This is all labor too. Why not, instead, do the work of healing, which is not easy or cute but can lead to wholeness and the community that comes with solidarity? The beginning of the healing journey can leave us feeling unmoored.

Imagination is central to activism. After decades of sex segregation, unequal funding and media coverage, and a horrendous record of harassment and abuse in sports keeping people apart, can you imagine a world where cis men, trans men, cis women, trans women, and gender expansive folks build a fairer sporting world for everyone? Can you imagine us creating the next iteration of Title IX together? Can we live our lives as if the future is already here?

"Queerness is not yet here," argues José Esteban Muñoz,

adding, "We are not yet queer. . . . Queerness is that thing that lets us feel that this world is not yet enough, that indeed something is missing."[69] The trans athletes we interviewed understand that the future is queerness's domain. By claiming and living into queerness, these athletes are generative and vital, waking us up to how a two-category sports system limits us all. Standing up as themselves in the middle of a straight, cis, sex-segregated system is what Muñoz may call "the Great Refusal" of queerness. It is a deep knowing that the present is not all there is, is not the end of the story.

Athletes are saying we have outgrown this system, and they can see a future where there are more expansive ways to live and play, a future brimming with potential, "a 'not-yet' where queer youths . . . actually get to grow up."[70] The current system is not enough. Trans and nonbinary athletes are asking us to look with them and see a more creative, vibrant sporting community. Once we see it, we can help them create it and live into it. To step out of the current system, we must see how it limits us. See how insufficient the current system is. Then we can feel the pull of queerness toward a place and time that is "fuller, vaster, more sensual, and brighter. From shared critical dissatisfaction we arrive at collective potentiality."[71]

One opportunity for disrupting gender hierarchies in sports is to question the binary system and consider the role of gender in sports. We can ask questions that do not reinforce the strict binary but offer bigger, more generative opportunities that support curiosity and wonder while honoring diverse bodies, like, What is gender? Why are men assumed to be superior? Why and how do we categorize athletes by gender? Instead of wondering if trans women should be included in sports, we can ask, Why do women's sports exist? Another way is possible.

CONCLUSION

THE MYTH THAT TRANS ATHLETES ARE COMING IN DROVES TO steal medals and do harm and must be stopped immediately to protect cis girls and women is compelling. Trans inclusion in sports is an emotionally charged issue, and many people have a stake in the game.

For folks fighting for trans inclusion, there is fear and pain. For folks fighting for trans exclusion, there is fear and pain. Many trans-inclusionary folks want everyone to have access to sports. Many trans-exclusionary folks don't want to lose the women's sports that they've fought hard for. They want to keep the scraps they have. Both feelings are valid, and interestingly, we believe, the reason for both is the same—we all want sports to offer more to girls and women (and boys and men). We want sports spaces that feel safe and free from toxicity. To get there, we must collectively validate one another's pain. We must also acknowledge that trans women are not perpetrators. We must acknowledge that trans advocates are not radicals and that trans-exclusionary activists are also not radicals. It is often the case that people on both sides of this alleged argument have been victims of violence, toxicity, and discrimination in sports. Many people, including men of color, boys from urban areas, trans athletes, and women have been.

When we look again, we see that sports as a system is inherently unfair. Some bodies are born with physical advantages for their sport, but they must also work hard and have access to the financial support, facilities, and coaching to be successful. It's important to recognize that physical advantage does not always translate to performance dominance, and every elite athlete has worked hard to maximize their potential. Let's acknowledge these inequalities and work to ensure that both cis and trans athletes can maximize their athletic potential, safely and without facing abuse.

Gender inequity still reigns in sports. Let's challenge the assumption that cis men are superior in sports. Ongoing sex segregation in sports perpetuates this assumption, and we must question the socialization processes that reinforce it. Women's sports are consistently underfunded and undervalued—why? We need to confront our biases about bodies, sex, and superiority. Let's work to support all girls and women so that they can have a more equitable sports experience.

Athletes like Laurel Hubbard and Lia Thomas and the lesser-known trans athletes you met in this book are not ruining the competitive landscape. They are not out to steal medals or do harm. The moral panic and restrictive policies around trans athletes are exaggerated and creating a culture that makes it feel dangerous for trans folks to be themselves. Trans kids, especially, who are afraid to come out or pursue sports are being harmed.

Instead of making society less safe for trans folks, sports can be an antidote for not just trans kids but all kids. Sports can help young people build critical life skills, including communication, teamwork, and leadership, while providing a community of peers to connect with and develop positive relationships with.[1] Young people who have access to sports consistently report better grades, better health, higher self-esteem, fewer risky behaviors, and a stronger belief in their abilities and competencies.[2]

By listening to trans athletes, reading up on the science of sex and gender, and asking better questions, we can have a more intelligent, thoughtful, complex, and humane conversation about trans inclusion and gender equity in sports. We can ask better, more nuanced and generative questions about fairness, safety, and gender equity. We can create informed, strategic policies that address safety and fairness for all athletes and that consider age, sport, and intensity level while promoting more pathways to participation in sports.

We also can't think our way out of a feeling problem. Yes, we must do our due diligence by reading, researching, and listening. We must get curious about science, be willing to sift for accurate information, and seek out people who have committed their lives to trans advocacy. We must think. However, if we are going to have humane conversations and write humane policies, we are going to have to turn toward our bodies, turn toward our feelings, and be honest about what we find there. Read the following passage and notice what happens in your body while you read the following:

> Let people affirm their sex. Let people affirm their gender. Let people use the facilities of their choosing when those choices are segregated. Give everyone access to holistic health care. Let athletes compete in the sex category with which they align. If and when trans girls win, allow it to mean that some girls are better at their sport than others, they performed well when it counted, and their hard work has paid off in this particular moment.

Where in your body did you sense constriction? Where did you have the urge to turn away, talk back, or argue, if at all? What stories, images, or sensations arose?

We know more and more about how healing happens. Many of us have healing to do around gender, and conversations and policymaking around trans athletes will be so much more humane if we are committed to our own healing and responsible for our own lives. If we can bring a regulated nervous system and self-awareness to the table, allowing our bodies and our feelings to be present with our minds and our thoughts, we can respond instead of react. We can offer nonviolent communication, collaboration, and dreaming and move toward a sports landscape that promotes gender equity. As Judith Butler reminds us, "Possibility is not a luxury; it is as crucial as bread."[3]

Banning trans athletes is affecting us all. Trans athletes—their experiences, insights, joy—can pave the way into a sports world that feels safer and more exuberant and is available to everybody. Organized sports can create a model for a more inclusive society for trans folks. In the work of gender equity in sports, trans joy is leading the way. Our society will be healthier and happier if more of us can live and move toward a sense of being at home in our bodies, being at home with ourselves, and being at home while playing sports. Our society would be a safer, more well place if more people really knew what it felt like to flow, to belong, to play, and to be free. That's the real win.

Let's come together to work for a sports culture where no one sex or gender or sexuality is superior to another or the norm. Let's build a world where, whenever possible, people of all genders have access to movement, play, and fair games. Let's promote and model moving, playing, and competing joyfully as a pathway toward collective freedom.

AUTHORS' NOTE

I, ELLIE, AM A CISGENDER WOMAN. I KNEW IT SUBCONSCIOUS-
ly, and now consciously. I started organized sports at age four
and played three sports in high school and two in college. I
started coaching at age fourteen and have continued working
with athletes to this day. I am also a teacher. I started teaching
in a high school classroom at age twenty-six and imagine I will
always teach in some capacity. All these pieces of me wake up
when we start to talk about transgender inclusion in sports.

In a sex-segregated sports world, which category do trans
athletes choose? Can trans athletes play and compete in the
gender category with which they align? One's entry point
into the conversation is pivotal. My entry point was a boy
named Mark.

Fifteen years before trans athletes became big news, a group
of tenth graders walked into my classroom for the first hour of

class on the first day of the school year. Mark was one of those students. Already well over a head taller than me as a sophomore, Mark had short hair and a deep voice and wore a boy's uniform. When I took attendance, I did a double take when I saw his name listed as Catherine. To me, Mark was a boy before he was a transgender boy. Then he was a boy *because* he was a transgender boy. Thus began a deeply meaningful relationship with my first trans student. He was smart, with a dry wit. He was good to his friends and was a whiz at theater lighting and props. He kindly corrected me if I misused any terminology related to his gender identity. I went to Mark's high school graduation party, where a baby picture of him in a pink dress was displayed next to his senior picture in a blue button up.

I went on to have several other trans students, some of whom came out and began transitioning in high school. For others, it happened later. Some had the support of their parents; others didn't. A high school classmate and softball teammate of mine transitioned when we were in our late thirties. My sister-in-law's child came out as trans at age ten.

When trans athletes became big news a few years back and bills restricting their participation and access to health care passed, it wasn't stories and ideas we were talking about, it was real people I cared about, people who were vulnerable and who needed and deserved advocacy. Cis folks were making policies restricting movement and play of people like Mark.

Whenever a bill is passed, I was taught to look to the most vulnerable people in society and wonder how the policy would affect them. From being in relationship with my trans students, friends, and nibling, instead of seeing these bills as protecting cis athletes, I see them as a detriment to trans athletes.[1] I see how we all lose by sidelining them. I see how scary and dangerous it can be for them to be out. I see the mental, emotional, and psychological strain on them as they navigate their sense of identity in a society designed for cis people. I also see the courage, beauty, and creativity they have, and from which I can learn. Moving toward advocacy for trans athletes, I had to recognize and contend with my cis privilege. Being a woman in a society where violence against women is tolerated makes me vulnerable, and being cis comes with its ease and protections. Both can be true. Advocating for girls and women in sports is paramount; I have been fighting for it as a female athlete and coach my whole life. It is clear to me that restricting trans athletes does not protect girls and women. It does the opposite.

I met Anna on a gender equity in sports panel before trans athletes became big news. We hit it off and stayed in touch. In my previous book, *The Embodied Path*, I interviewed several trans folks and was enamored with their embodied stories of identity and becoming. I kept moving my work into body stories and narrative repair. When Anna read the book, she reached out and asked me to join her in her work on trans rights so we could weave narratives of trans athletes in with her research and write collaboratively from our throats, using our heads and our hearts. This project invited me to step into my role as a trans ally more officially. Over the course of creating this book, we sought truth and became together.

I, Dr. Anna Baeth, had a different entry point to the conversation. I began my career as a collegiate field hockey coach in 2009. In 2011, the state of Massachusetts had a Title IX ruling that allowed high school cis boys to compete on the girls' teams. Field hockey is one of the few sports in the United States that was developed by and for women and where women maintain most leadership positions, and I felt deeply protective of it. A graduate of an all-women's institution, I believed in the power of women-only spaces. Would allowing cis boys to participate harm the experiences of cis girls? This same argument is used to limit the play of trans girls and women. For me, transgender girls participating in women's sport felt a lot like cis boys participating in women's sport. When I fought for women-only spaces, I initially meant only cis women.

I have since coached five trans athletes and found that they were all college-aged humans doing college-aged human activities—pulling stunts, trying to get better at a sport, learning how to be good teammates, and mostly just trying to find themselves. I became a quiet advocate for my trans athletes.

Then my father died, and I had to learn to be vulnerable in front of my athletes. In my grief, I cried in front of them and even had a panic attack on the sidelines. My athletes—all of them, cis and trans—followed me toward vulnerability. We learned to breathe together. We learned to not fear or hurry our tears. Together, we felt how laughter springs from the same well as sorrow does.

When I started to be asked to speak on behalf of trans athletes in my role at Athlete Ally, I needed to figure out what I thought. In the latter half of 2020, I read every study I could find on transgender and intersex athletes, on testosterone, and on other categorical differences between elite, trained male athletes and elite, trained female athletes. I skimmed nearly three thousand media articles about transgender athletes and reached out to forty-two endocrinologists to ask them to speak with me about the impacts of testosterone on athletic performance. I reached out to several key academics in the disciplines of sport psychology, sport sociology, and cultural studies to understand their thoughts and perspectives on the state of trans identity in sport, what work had been done, and what work might to be done in this space by a cis ally. As I learned more, I became a stronger ally and advocate for trans athletes. Meanwhile, I was also becoming a scholar, a coach, and a Quaker. These identities intertwined with becoming a trans ally.

In 2021, anti-transness spiked in sport spaces and in ways never seen before, and an interest in trans athletes became a focal point in the academy. It was a perfect storm that allowed me to examine what I thought I knew about gender and socialization in sport, to study the science behind athletic performance and sex, to meet trans athletes, to incorporate queerness into my research, and to become allied with the trans community. Joy kept me in coaching and pushed me to active activism for trans athletes. My work as a coach and scholar has brought me to believe that supporting girls and women undeniably means supporting trans athletes, loudly when necessary. We all win when we all win.

I, Dr. Baeth, am a cis, white, queer woman and a Quaker.

I, Ellie, am a cis, white, queer woman. We are both highly educated, able-bodied, and neurotypical. These identities offer us inherent privileges, including having access to our bodies since childhood. We are athletes. We love activity and being in our bodies, and we have thrived in sport spaces. We both love our bodies and are fascinated by bodies. It all kicked open the door to allyship, and we feel deeply that walking through that door is what will make us free. Trans athletes need allies. As cis people, we seriously questioned whether it was appropriate for us to be speaking up and out on behalf of the trans community, until we saw the numbers and until we saw the strain on trans bodies to simply stay safe in our country.

We believe cis white women are rightfully accused of lacking stamina and resiliency when it comes to allyship. We believe to build stamina and resilience, the work needs to happen in a joyful community, and we each benefit from practices that metabolize anger and embrace rest. We see wellness as different from self-care in that it addresses burnout in community and equips us for sustained action. And we see the grit culture that white supremacy perpetuates as a barrier to allyship. Folks feel too busy, overwhelmed, isolated, anxious, exhausted, and afraid to care and act. As Audre Lorde writes, "And the speaking will get easier and easier. . . . And you will lose some friends and lovers and realize you don't miss them. And new ones will find you and cherish you. . . . And at last you'll know with surpassing certainty that only one thing is more frightening than speaking your truth. And that is not speaking."[2]

Just because it is less common to be trans does not mean that it is less normal. Just because it is more common to be cis does not mean it is more normal. Ultimately, given the very low number of trans athletes and our position as cis athletes, our hope is to engender a deeper understanding of gender dysphoria for ourselves and among potential trans supporters and to create pathways for such allyship. We believe allyship is the "active, consistent, and arduous practice of unlearning and re-evaluating, in which a person in a position of privilege and power seeks to operate in solidarity with a marginalized group."[3] It requires a lifelong reckoning with one's own privilege. There is a long history of privileged bodies thinking they are doing the work of allyship, defining themselves as moral while in fact perpetuating oppressive systems. Allyship, then, takes on components of resistance, risk taking and sacrifice, accountability and collaboration, decentering and intersectionality.

Because it is relational, it is messy and hard to quantify. It is full of good conflict. It is queer. As with all queer formations, allyship is permeable and mutable and evolving—not a singular moment or identity but a lifelong process.[4]

We believe the components of allyship include the following:

1. A lifelong and active praxis of seeking and becoming
2. A need for proximity or being in community with people holding minoritized identities
3. A reckoning with one's own privilege
4. The knowledge that allyship or one's vision of social justice might never be realized.[5]

Seeking and becoming feels much like rhizomes: "an underground—but perfectly manifest—network of multiple branching roots and shoots, with no central axis, no unified point of origin, and no given direction of growth—a proliferating, somewhat chaotic, and diversified system".[6] We view allyship as a rhizomatic process in which one's thinking is explored and expanded via interactive experiences—experiences that bump up against and intertwine with systems, other people, other bodies, and our own bodies—that we use to elucidate our journeys as allies, which has never been linear, progressive, or ending. Rather, allyship has come in fits and starts through rhizomatic ponderings, interactions, and data, or becoming. Like our trans siblings, we too are becoming. Becoming is not a linear progression but a changing at the level of being rather than simply a changing of state. Becoming allied is a reflexive and arduous praxis of integrating relationships, behaviors, and beliefs.

Allyship calls us away from indifference into action, moving from tolerance and acceptance to nurturance. It is not only believing trans people when they tell us who they are but also working for policies and procedures at the institutional and systemic level that will remove barriers to their thriving. Dr. Dorothy Riddle created a psychometric scale in 1973–74 to measure the degree that someone is homophobic. The Riddle Scale is still used today. The categories from bottom to top are repulsion, pity, tolerance, acceptance, support, admiration, appreciation, and nurturance. Allyship exists in the top half of the scale, when people are consistently opting into the work of admiring, appreciating, and nurturing folks whom society casts as others. It requires listening, unlearning, learning, and acting. We gained deep admiration and appreciation for the participants in this book, and we trust that you did too.

All the participants in this book are inordinately brave. When we initially solicited requests for interviewees for this book, we had asked adult trans athletes to tell us their stories. Yet, we heard again and again from parents and athletes under seventeen—some as young as eight—who wanted to tell their stories, to share them with the world in the face of terrifying legislation. This gave us hope and imbued us with a deep sense of responsibility to young trans athletes across the United States.

We are cis and only theoretically understand gender euphoria, which is the experience of elation, satisfaction, or joy when your experience of gender aligns with your gender identity instead of the gender you were assigned at birth. It's not something we think about often in everyday life. But what we do understand, theoretically and physically, is sport. We are athletes and coaches, and like many coaches, there is nothing quite as joyful as being with an athlete when they accomplish something new for the first time, or at the right time. When they've been practicing a skill for weeks and, finally, they can do it during a competition—that is coaching joy. It's sweet, funny, heart-screaming, jump-up-and-down joy. And when we read joy like that on a person, we start to hum with it too. Trans joy came up so often in our interviews that it could not be ignored. We believe trans joy can lead us all into a better sports world, where all bodies feel free to move, grow, and play.

APPENDIX A: SUGGESTED PATHWAYS TO PLAY

Trans athletes wanting to play in the gender category they align with gives us an opportunity to reconsider how we *do* sports. Instead of taking advantage of that opportunity to build a sports culture that is more inclusive and equitable, we have done the opposite. Experts who do work around hormones, sex, competitive advantage, and performance, and know what they are doing, are not consulted on policies as they pertain to trans athletes. Trans athletes themselves are underutilized as well. We would like to see experts and trans athletes at the policy tables helping to create smart, relevant, inclusive policies that lead to more athletes being able to play, instead of fewer. A new way forward is possible.

The myths that conservative policymakers and anti-trans advocates perpetuate are framed as absolute and universal. They state that *all* the trans athletes are coming in droves and *all* are stealing medals, doing harm, and ruining women's sports. Thus, they *all* need to be banned from participating, always, completely, and immediately. The myths are appealing to some because of their simplicity and clarity. Yet just because the message is simple and clear, it does not make it accurate, helpful, strategic, or right. In reality, bodies and sports are much too nuanced and complex for absolutes. Good, savvy, science-based, supportive policy that creates pathways to participation will vary depending on the sport, the age level, and the intensity level. These policies, too, need to be nuanced and complex. Most trans athletes want to play and compete at a very low-stakes game. As the stakes change, so can inclusive policies.

For trans kids, we have to give them time and space to explore their identities without rushing them into a binary so that they can play. Puberty happens at different times for different kids, and neither the kids nor their parents, guardians, or coaches want to rush their identity formation and decisions to begin gender-affirming hormone treatment. There is simply no good science yet on competitive advantage for trans youths. Because of human variance, universal policies across ages, levels, and sports for kids do not seem possible. But one thing is clear: Any policy that regulates trans youth athletes should center kids' mental and physical health and encourage their participation—instead of hyper-focusing on them winning.

To create a fair, safe, and inclusive sports environment for kids, let's keep youth sports free when possible. Keep sports sex integrated through elementary school. In high school, let athletes choose the category where they feel aligned. Make locker rooms and sports spaces safer for all kids and make health care support available to all kids.

Sports are vital for young people's physical and mental health; participation barriers must be removed. We ensure that all kids benefit from sports by reducing costs, providing better facilities, and encouraging supportive coaches and team belonging. Trans and gender-expansive youths should not be required to undergo medical interventions to play sports comfortably. They deserve a supportive environment to explore their identities. As sports become segregated, we must combat harmful stereotypes about certain bodies being inferior and support all athletes in retaining confidence and joy. The system should serve the holistic development of all young athletes, not intensify the exclusion of some.

Kids are claiming their rights to their bodies. Trans kids are asking to be safe and legal and to be able to play safely and legally. They are asking for free will to make choices about who they are. Adults are looking for good research to help kids navigate school, sports, and health care systems created for cis kids, and finding it lacking. It is understandable that some adults, even caring parents, coaches, and administrators, are a little anxious. Most of us feel underinformed about things like puberty blockers and gender-affirming health care, and the stakes feel high, especially if we feel responsible for the well-being and safety of the kids coming out.[1] Some adults may think kids coming out as trans are succumbing to a fad. Some adults point to depression, social media, and a desire to fit in or stand out. Some adults worry about regret later in life. It is helpful to name our discomfort, keep asking for good research, move at the speed of trust, and listen to how kids are experiencing life in their bodies. People look to sports and athletes to represent values that the rest of society should live by. We have an opportunity to join other facets of society that model acceptance and celebrate trans athletes. We can tell all kids that they matter, that they deserve support and care, and that our teams are better with them on it. Sports are not separate from society. The way we understand gender and sex is shifting dramatically. As more and more young people identify as trans, gender expansive, and nonbinary, they look for a place to belong. Sport communities have an opportunity to catch up and open to the benefit of all participants.

In recreational sports, trans women, trans men, intersex, nonbinary, and gender expansive people should be able to participate where they feel most comfortable. Allow trans athletes to speak for themselves—include them in conversations about trans athletes. Eliminate gendered categories and rules where possible, question assumptions about language, and create teams and leagues that are explicitly safe and queer.

There is no need to restrict trans athletes from low-stakes sports. Recreational sports should be about having fun, sustaining lifelong fitness, and building community, not about being exclusive. We can create more integrated sports opportunities where gender and sex are irrelevant, focusing instead on the joy of movement and play. Like Ciara, a trans athlete we interviewed, said, "I think it's a misconception to apply the Olympic model to all of sport. That ignores all the other equally important functions that sport plays in society. Fostering acceptance, and teaching teamwork, and independence, self-confidence. All those other great lessons that sport teaches in its unique way. I think yes, absolute performance is an important consideration, but it shouldn't drown out those other considerations."

For trans men at the NCAA and IOC level, have sport-specific policy that creates a pathway to participation. Trans men and nonbinary individuals should have the freedom to play recreational and elite sports in the category that aligns with their identity, without having to disclose their gender. Let's not conflate gender-affirming hormone treatment with doping. Our current sports system often overlooks trans men and nonbinary athletes, who deserve recognition and inclusion. At the elite level, sport-specific policies that account for different needs, such as those undergoing gender-affirming hormone treatment, can ensure fairness and inclusivity.[2]

For women at the NCAA and IOC level, athletes assigned female at birth with high naturally occurring testosterone should be able to compete in the female category. Let's ban fear-based, invasive, single-factor tests to determine the sex of athletes, and instead create science-based policy on doping and gender-affirming hormone treatment and write policy that creates safe pathways toward participation for trans women that make sense for the sport.

At the elite level, physical characteristics only get you so far. Technical skill, coaching, mental toughness, grit, pain tolerance, ability to heal from injury, luck, timing, and facilities matter greatly. Every person's body is different. Becoming an

elite athlete is incredibly difficult, with many factors contributing to success. While regulations around doping are understandable, trans women should be allowed to compete under
guidelines that recognize the complexity of athletic advantage beyond hormone levels. Athletes assigned female at birth
and who have higher natural testosterone levels should not
be excluded from competition. Sport-specific policy for trans
women makes sense in elite sports, but invasive testing or body
policing should be avoided, and a one-size-fits-all approach is
inappropriate.

Bans and restrictions on trans athletes are sidelining athletes, increasing sanctioned gender policing, intensifying a culture of skepticism around being trans, and creating a culture of
fear in sports that is harming cis and trans athletes alike. We
have an opportunity to shift sports so that it can lead the way
in dismantling gender inequity instead of contributing to it,
and we have the experts to help us get there. Now is the time
to listen to experts and trans athletes to create better policies
and to shift toward a more inclusive sports culture where all
athletes can play.

APPENDIX B: TEN BETTER QUESTIONS CIS FOLKS CAN ASK EACH OTHER

1. Can you tell me about your experience being cisgender?
2. When you talk about someone's gender and sex, what do you mean?
3. What, if anything, bothers you about the idea of trans athletes competing in sports? Where does the rub come from? Where do you feel it in your body?
4. Why are men assumed to be superior athletes? If you learned that, when, how, and from whom?
5. Why and how do we categorize athletes by gender? Why do women's sports exist?
6. Why do so few institutions in this country comply with Title IX? Why do women's sports get so much less support, media coverage, and pay than men's?
7. Why is violence against girls and women so high in

sports? Who is being harmed and by whom in sports? Who is safer and who is more at risk?

8. Who is benefiting financially from restricting trans kids and adults from playing?

9. Why do Black and brown girls have less access to resources and drop out of sports at double the rate compared with their white, wealthy, suburban counterparts? How can we better support all bodies to play?

10. How can we remove cost as a barrier so that more kids can play sports?

APPENDIX C:
RECOMMENDED RESOURCES

Amateur: A True Story About What Makes a Man by Thomas Page McBee

Believed podcast by NPR and Michigan Public Radio

Changing the Game documentary (2019)

Deconstructing the Fitness Industrial Complex: How to Resist, Disrupt, and Reclaim What It Means to Be Fit in American Culture, edited by Justice Roe Williams, Roc Rochon, and Lawrence Koval

Fair Play: How Sports Shape the Gender Debates by Katie Barnes

Inciting Joy: Essays by Ross Gay

Let Them Play, Self magazine, self.com/package/let-them-play

Make It Count: My Fight to Become the First Transgender Olympic Runner by CeCé Telfer

My Grandmother's Hands: Racialized Trauma and the Pathway to Mending Our Hearts and Bodies by Resmaa Menakem

Open Play: The Case for Feminist Sport by Sheree Bekker and Stephen Mumford

The Other Olympian: Fascism, Queerness, and the Making of Modern Sports by Michael Waters

Queer Phenomenology: Orientations, Objects, Others by Sara Ahmed

The Race to Be Myself: A Memoir by Caster Semenya

The Sum of Us: What Racism Costs Everyone and How We Can Prosper Together by Heather McGhee

Tested podcast by NPR and CBC

Testosterone: An Unauthorized Biography by Rebecca Jordan-Young and Katrina Karkazis

The Tragedy of Heterosexuality by Jane Ward

Transathlete.com, website by Chris Mosier, transathlete.com

Who's Afraid of Gender? by Judith Butler

ACKNOWLEDGMENTS

Our first thank you goes to the participants in this project. Thank you for stepping forward with courage, vulnerability, and trust. Thank you for sharing your stories. Thank you for seeing the world you want to live in and creating it by living authentically day in and day out.

Chris Mosier, you are the adult we all needed when we were kids. You are the man we still need as adults. This project would not have happened without you. Thank you for your tireless advocacy for trans athletes, and for making the way by walking, running, and biking it. You interviewed the kids with deep care and wisdom. We are so grateful. A deep thanks goes out to Ali Greey, who joined us in the early brainstorming of this book and in the process of interviewing the athletes. Thank you to Jen Larrick, Jess Braverman, Kevin Lally, Claire Bischoff, and Pat Roscher for being early expert readers and giving such stellar feedback. You shaped the book for the better. Thank you to the wildly talented Erin White, who pushed in all the right places to make the project proposal shine.

We are endlessly grateful to our agent, Stephanie Rostan. Thank you for believing in and advocating for us and our project with such clear expertise and passion, head and heart. And to our editor, zakia henderson-brown, you saw us and the project right away and strengthened it at every turn. You and the whole team at The New Press made for collaboration at its best.

I, Chris, want to thank every athlete who trusted us with their stories; it's a privilege and a responsibility we don't take lightly. Thank you to the families, parents, and guardians of the youth we spoke with for supporting your child and allowing them to share their perspectives. And thank you to Zhen Heinemann for their enthusiastic support of all my endeavors.

I, Ellie, am overwhelmingly grateful for my writing community. Sally Franson, thank you for always being my friend first, for teaching me so much about courage, healing, and love, for naming me auntie, demanding I stand up for and believe in myself, sharing your therapist, and reminding me that the emperor has no clothes. Laura Fanucci, thank you for holding the lantern for me and being my soul companion as we keep building multi-vocational erotic lives. How wonderful to be alive and do this work alongside you. Laura, Stina Kielsmeier-Cook, and Shannon Evans, my best writing happened at the cabin, and my bravest moments came to being with your love and support buoying me. Brian Benson, thank you for writing your story so powerfully that it invites me to do the same. Molly and Marchaé, thank you for the gift of your time and care in our writing group. Meta, Natalia, and Matthew, your joy and collaboration are a balm to my dry bones. Thank you for dreaming with me and seeing that a better world is on its way. Sam, keep puking and sifting and crafting beautiful poems. You make the journey fuller and richer. And to the brilliant Plum writers—Andi, Steph, Julie, Taylor, Hanna, Jackie, Kiely, Sue, Mary Jo, Shoshana, Alyssa, and Nicole—time reading, breathing, and creating with you nourishes me and brings me so much connection and joy. You help keep the pilot light of hope and beauty burning. Anna, same hand soul friend, thank you for being brave, for slaying your dragons, facing your fears, finding your voice, using your power, and partnering me so well in all the ways. We're just getting started.

I'd like to thank Mark, Drew, Lauren, Sawyer, Myrtle, Cameron, Chris, Ali, Heather, and Jake for your patience with me on the journey and for inspiring me with your courage and embodied freedom. You ever so gently invited me to come out as cis and with grace and pizazz and modeled how to dismantle the systems that stymie us. Juliet, thanks for always capturing my good side and inviting me to claim my lane. Emma, thank you for helping me bravely step up to take my seat. To my therapists, Nicole and Jenna, thank you for holding space for me to do the hard work of healing so that I could bring more of my true essence and an open, curious heart to this project.

Writing this was an invitation to circle back to my childhood, which was saturated in sports. I am grateful to grow up in a sports family and have my embodied life supported so deeply. Thank you to my family, coaches, and teammates who loved me in all my intensity and competitiveness as well as in moments of brokenness and defeat. You supported me claiming my autonomy and power before I was conditioned to know any better, and I am still benefiting from that today.

This book required that I step out of line and be disobedient, which requires audacity and repatterning for me. Laura, Hanna, Sally, Anna, Molly, and Chrissy, thank you for loving me back and leaping to grab the mirror when you saw glimpses of liberation cross over my face. Kev, our work remains integral to this, and you are such a valued thought partner and heart friend.

When I emerge from my cave, my found family is always there, holding me up, embracing me, welcoming me back. Thank you to my Up Yoga family, EP4 Decadent Club, the Wonder Women, my book soulmate and dancing queen Meghan, my soul friend Jennifer, the Collegeville Institute community, the Rise Rooted crew, and Craig, Betsy, Ellen, and Tessa, my Marco buds, for tethering me to goodness, life, and love.

Dan, I *might* be able to write without your co-parenting, life-partnering, and behind-the-scenes-support, but it wouldn't be pretty. Thank you for always committing, albeit sometimes overcommitting, to the space it requires for me to expand, love, create, and build a multifaceted life. Simon and Miles, it still brings me to a hushed, teary awe that I get to be your momma. It continues to be my very favorite thing to be. Your imagination expands our home and our lives. Loving you and being loved by you is one of my great romances, and writing books alongside you is heaven.

I, Anna, am humbled and grateful by the many people who have loved and supported me personally and professionally. Foremost, I have been incredibly lucky to be in the company of smart, kind, thoughtful colleagues who have given me new lenses through which to see the world. AC, Joanna, Gio, T, Hudson, Jaspreet, Ryan, Jo, Sam, Leo, and, especially, AJ.

I want to thank the scholars and advocates who have also supported me along the way. Shane, Cheryl, Casey, Libby, Jaime, Lindsay, Adam, Doug, Jane, Travers, Roc, Anna P., Anna G., Anna B., Liz, the list goes on and on—the traces of all of you are all over this book.

To Danne Diamond and Chris Mosier, I don't know how you both do it—your magic, thoughtfulness, and care continue to astonish me. You never compromise your values. Not just in your passion for the work but in the ways you treat all people with kindness and dignity. This world is lucky to have you and you continue to inspire me to live and act with integrity and love.

To my coaching colleagues, Gina, Jac, Jill, Kenen, Andy, and the entire MHC field hockey staff, you continuously help me see how sports can be done differently. To all of my current and former athletes, thank you for the daily reminders of why this work matters.

To my PLP, Kelley, thank you for helping me to see this as yet another of life's adventures. Sara, Grandma Dean, the Baeth clan, Joey, Lauri, Val, John, and Kelsey (and Nia and

P!), and one of the strongest women I know, Mom, I would not have made it to see this book to its publication without you. Dad, I wish you were here to celebrate over a root beer float.

Katlin, my life would be irrevocably different without you. Thank you for the endless support, laughter, and love over the years.

KiKi, thank you for reminding me of who I am. Thank you for the hundreds of cups of coffee and walking talks. You've done more to support the well-being of diverse athletes than most people will ever know. Let's face it, I am undone by you, and I can't imagine it otherwise.

Finally, to Ellie—one of the greatest loves of my life. You have been with me in the fear, in the grief, and in the pain. You have been with me through the giggles, laughter, and energies of this book. And you have consistently reminded me of the sheer joy that comes with freedom. My famous friend, you know how to push me, love me, and run with me. I am thankful you've been willing to do so. I remain in awe of you and can't wait for our next plutonic honeymoon.

NOTES

Introduction

1. **Gender identity** is one's core sense of being a woman, a man, some of both, or neither. We all have a gender identity and a felt sense of gender identity, including cis people. Awareness of gender identity is usually experienced early in life, but it may also shift over the course of one's life. See Lyne Chiniara, "Gender Identity," *Medscape*, June 26, 2023, www .medscape.com/article/2552242-overview; Chris Mosier, "Trans Terminology," Transathlete, www.transathlete.com/starthere; Laurel Wamsley, "A Guide to Gender Identity Terms," NPR, June 2, 2021, www.npr .org/sections/health-shots/2021/06/02/994089002/a-guide-to-gender -identity-terms. A person's **sex assigned at birth** is the sex that is assigned to an infant at birth, usually by a doctor or medical staff, based on the infant's visible anatomy, including genitalia and other physical characteristics. Sex assigned at birth is most often male, female, or intersex. See "Children and Gender Identity: Supporting Your Child," *Mayo Clinic*, October 1, 2022, www.mayoclinic.org/healthy-lifestyle/childrens -health/in-depth/children-and-gender-identity/art-20266811; Mosier, "Trans Terminology."

2. Some people are **transgender**—an umbrella term used to describe people whose gender identity differs from their sex assigned at birth. Transgender people span all communities and come from a variety of backgrounds, ethnicities, ages, and abilities. There is no one single transgender experience, just like not all cisgender people are the same. Transgender is sometimes shortened to *trans*. See "Understanding Transgender People, Gender Identity and Gender Expression," *American Psychological Association*, June 6, 2023, www.apa.org/topics/lgbtq/transgender-people-gender-identity-gender-expression; Mosier, "Trans Terminology"; Wamsley, "Gender Identity Terms." Historically, people have thought of transgender people as making a binary transition, meaning transitioning from female to male or male to female; in fact, this is reflected in outdated language like FTM (female-to-male) or MTF (male-to-female). While many trans people do make transitions that fit more neatly within society's expectations of typical gender roles, a growing number of people are finding comfort in pushing back on the binary system altogether. See Joanna Harper, *Sporting Gender: The History, Science, and Stories of Transgender and Intersex Athletes* (Rowman & Littlefield, 2019).

3. Anna Baeth and Ellie Roscher, *Queering Populism, Sport, and Isolationism: What Is Happening with Transgender Athletes and What It Says About Us* (Rutgers University Press, forthcoming); Anna Baeth and Anna Goorevich, "Mediated Moral Panics: Trans Athlete Spectres, the Haunting of Cisgender Girls and Politicians as Moral Entrepreneurs in 2021," in *Justice for Trans Athletes, Challenges and Struggles*, ed. Ali Durham Greey and Heather Jefferson Lenskyj (Emerald, 2022), 137–49.

4. Laura Meckler, "Biden Title IX Rules on Trans Athletes Set for Election-Year Delay," *Washington Post*, March 28, 2024; Brooke Migdon, "Trump Vows to Reverse Transgender Student Protections 'On Day One,'" *The Hill*, May 10, 2024.

5. Erin Reed, "Anti-Trans Legislative Risk Assessment Map: July 2024 Edition," *Erin in the Morning*, www.erininthemorning.com/p/anti-trans-legislative-risk-assessment-3dc.

6. Baeth and Goorevich, "Mediated Moral Panics."

7. Baeth and Roscher, *Queering Populism*.

8. Baeth and Roscher, *Queering Populism*.

1. Who Are Trans Athletes?

1. Anna Baeth and Ellie Roscher, *Queering Populism, Sport, and Isolationism: What Is Happening with Transgender Athletes and What It Says About Us* (Rutgers University Press, forthcoming).

2. Anna Baeth and Anna Goorevich, "Mediated Moral Panics: Trans Athlete Spectres, the Haunting of Cisgender Girls and Politicians as Moral Entrepreneurs in 2021," in *Justice for Trans Athletes, Challenges and Struggles*, ed. Ali Durham Greey and Heather Jefferson Lenskyj (Emerald, 2022), 137–49.

3. Baeth and Goorevich, "Mediated Moral Panics."

4. International Olympic Committee, "Fairness, Inclusion and Non-Discrimination in Olympic Sport," www.olympics.com/ioc/human-rights/fairness-inclusion-nondiscrimination.

5. Chris Mosier and Danne Lieberman, "Trans and Nonbinary Inclusion in College Sports—101," Virtual training hosted by Athlete Ally and Transathlete.com, April 19, 2023.

6. Mosier and Lieberman, "Trans and Nonbinary Inclusion."

7. Shannon Scovel, Monica Nelson, and Holly Thorpe, "Media Framings of the Transgender Athlete as 'Legitimate Controversy': The Case of Laurel Hubbard at the Tokyo Olympics," *Communication & Sport* 11, no. 5 (2023): 838–53.

8. Movement Advancement Project, "Equality Maps: Bans on Transgender Youth Participation in Sports, www.mapresearch.org/equality-maps/youth/sports_participation_bans.

9. Anna Brown, "About 5% of Young Adults in the U.S. Say Their Gender Is Different from Their Sex Assigned at Birth," *Pew Research Center*, June 7, 2022, www.pewresearch.org/short-reads/2022/06/07/about-5-of-young-adults-in-the-u-s-say-their-gender-is-different-from-their-sex-assigned-at-birth.

10. Anna Baeth, Susie Poore, Adam Love, and Christina Friebott, "Representation Matter(s): Visibility Politics and Mediated Coverage of LGBTQI+ Athletes in 2021," *Communication & Sport*, forthcoming.

11. National Women's Law Center, "Reproductive Rights Include

Bodily Autonomy for Trans and Intersex Youth," National Women's Law Center Resources, August 9, 2022.

12. Alejandra Caraballo and Heron Greenesmith, "The Narrative on Trans Rights Is Being Shaped by Right-Wing Media," *Teen Vogue*, March 17, 2022. Movement Advancement Project, "Bans on Transgender Youth Participation in Sport" and "Bans on Best Practice Medical Care for Transgender Youth," www.mapresearch.org/equality-maps/healthcare /youth_medical_care_bans.

13. Shoshana K. Goldberg, "Fair Play: The Importance of Sports Participation for Transgender Youth," *Center for American Progress*, February 2021, www.americanprogress.org/article/fair-play.

14. Goldberg, "Fair Play."

15. Anna Baeth and Ellie Roscher, *Queering Populism, Sport, and Isolationism: What Is Happening with Transgender Athletes and What It Says About Us* (Rutgers University Press, forthcoming).

16. Movement Advancement Project and GLSEN, "Separation and Stigma: Transgender Youth and School Facilities," GLSEN, www.glsen .org/research/separation-and-stigma-transgender-youth-and-school -facilities.

17. Elizabeth Levy Paluck and Chelsey S. Clark, "Can Playing Together Help Us Live Together?" *Science*, 369 (August 2020): 769–70.

18. Goldberg, "Fair Play."

19. Movement Advancement Project, "Equality Maps: Bans on Transgender Youth Participation in Sports."

20. Movement Advancement Project, "Equality Maps: Bans on Best Practice Medical Care for Transgender Youth," 2024, and "Equality Maps: Bans on Transgender Youth Participation in Sports."

21. Movement Advancement Project and GLSEN, "Separation and Stigma."

22. Trevor Project, *2023 U.S. National Survey on the Mental Health of LGBTQ Young People*, www.thetrevorproject.org/survey-2023.

23. **Transitioning** is the process people take to affirm their identity, and it can take a multitude of forms. There's no singular way to transition

and no "right" way to transition; transitioning is deeply personal. There are many potential parts of a transition, including making a social transition (changing one's name, pronouns, clothing/style expression, and the facilities one uses); a medical transition (such as taking hormones or having gender-affirming surgeries); and/or a legal transition (changing documents such as identification cards, social security card, passport, and birth certificate). Many individuals choose not to, or are unable to, transition for a range of reasons, both personal and beyond their control. The validity of an individual's gender identity does not depend on any social, legal, and/or medical transition; the self-identification itself is what validates the gender identity. Many people consider transitioning to be a lifelong process, while others will exclusively refer to the beginning of their social or medical transition as when they transitioned. See Chris Mosier, "Trans Terminology," Transathlete, www.transathlete.com/starthere.

24. James Baldwin, "Notes on the House of Bondage," *The Nation*, November 1, 1980.

25. Dionne L. Koller, "Putting Public Law into 'Private' Sport," *Pepperdine Law Review* 43 (2015): 681.

26. Emily Fox, "Fairness for All? The Implications of Adopting a Third-Gender Category in Elite Sports," *Washington University Law Review* 101 (2023): 1373.

27. Jenna Weiner, "The New USAUT Trans Policy," *Skyd Magazine*, November 14, 2018.

28. Baeth, Poore, Love, and Friebott, "Representation Matter(s)."

2. Is It Unfair for Trans Athletes to Compete?

1. Rebecca M. Jordan-Young and Katrina Karkazis, *Testosterone: An Unauthorized Biography* (Harvard University Press, 2019).

2. Jordan-Young and Karkazis, *Testosterone*.

3. Jordan-Young and Karkazis, *Testosterone*; and J.E. Sumerau, "A Tale of Three Spectrums: Deviating from Normative Treatments of Sex and Gender," *Deviant Behavior* 41, no. 7 (2020): 893–904.

4. Nina N. Powell-Hamilton, "Overview of Sex Chromosome

Abnormalities," *Merck Manuals Consumer Version*, November 2023, www .merckmanuals.com/home/children-s-health-issues/chromosome-and -gene-abnormalities/overview-of-sex-chromosome-abnormalities.

5. Rosa Fernández et al., "Molecular Basis of Gender Dysphoria: Androgen and Estrogen Receptor Interaction," *Psychoneuroendocrinology* 98 (2018): 161–67.

6. Ferdinand J.O. Boucher and Tudor I. Chinnah, "Gender Dysphoria: A Review Investigating the Relationship Between Genetic Influences and Brain Development," *Adolescent Health, Medicine and Therapeutics* 11 (2020): 89–99.

7. Louis J. Elsas et al., "Gender Verification of Female Athletes," *Genetics in Medicine* 2, no. 4 (2000): 249–54; Roger Pielke Jr., "Sugar, Spice and Everything Nice: How to End 'Sex Testing' in International Athletics," *International Journal of Sport Policy and Politics* 9, no. 4 (2017): 649–65; Francisco J. Sánchez, Maria Jose Martínez-Patiño, and Eric Vilain, "The New Policy on Hyperandrogenism in Elite Female Athletes Is Not About 'Sex Testing,'" *Journal of Sex Research* 50, no. 2 (2013): 112–15.

8. Women's Sports Policy Working Group, "Don't Some Healthy Females Produce Testosterone in the 'Male' Range?" Women's Sport Working Group, March 26, 2025, womenssportspolicy.org/q10-dont -some-healthy-females-produce-testosterone-in-the-male-range.

9. Peter Sönksen, "Determination and Regulation of Body Composition in Elite Athletes," *British Journal of Sports Medicine* 52, no. 4 (2018): 219–29.

10. "Usain Bolt: A Woman Would Beat Me Over 800m," *Channel 5 News*, September 19, 2013, www.youtube.com/watch?v=veSqmr-HIWs.

11. Alan M. Nevill et al., "The Relative Contributions of Anaerobic and Aerobic Energy Supply During Track 100-, 400- and 800-m Performance," *Journal of Sports Medicine and Physical Fitness* 48, no. 2 (2008): 138–42.

12. **Cisgender people** are those whose gender identity is the same as the sex they were assigned at birth. Cisgender is often shortened to *cis*. See Chris Mosier, "Trans Terminology," Transathlete, www.transathlete.com /starthere; Laurel Wamsley, "A Guide to Gender Identity Terms," NPR,

June 2, 2021, www.npr.org/sections/health-shots/2021/06/02/994089002 /a-guide-to-gender-identity-terms.

13. Donald Padgett, "Michael Phelps Weighs In on Lia Thomas Controversy," *Out Magazine*, January 19, 2022.

14. Adam Hadhazy, "What Makes Michael Phelps So Good?" *Scientific American*, August 18, 2008.

15. Jordan-Young and Karkazis, *Testosterone*; Schultz et al., "The Future of Women's Sport Includes Transgender Women and Girls," in *Justice for Trans Athletes*, ed. Ali Durham Greey and Helen Lenskyj (Emerald, 2022), 17–29; and Travers, "'Female' Sport and Testosterone Panic," in *Justice for Trans Athletes: Challenges and Struggles*, ed. Ali Durham Greey and Helen Lenskyj (Emerald, 2022), 45–60.

16. Jordan-Young and Karkazis, *Testosterone*, 42.

17. Peter Sönksen, "Determination and Regulation of Body Composition in Elite Athletes," *British Journal of Sports Medicine* 52, no. 4 (2018): 219–29.

18. Daryl Adair and Peter Sönksen, "Fair Play at the Olympics: Testosterone and Female Athletes," *The Conversation*, June 21, 2016, theconversation.com/fair-play-at-the-olympics-testosterone-and-female-athletes -60156.

19. Jordan-Young and Karkazis, *Testosterone*.

20. All people have both **estrogen** and testosterone, but estrogen is typically higher in cis women and testosterone is typically higher in cis men (see Jordan-Young and Karkazis, *Testosterone*). Estrogen occurs naturally but is also used as medication in menopausal hormone treatment, hormonal birth control, and gender-affirming hormone treatment for trans women. Testosterone occurs naturally and is used to treat hypogonadism and breast cancer and as gender-affirming hormone treatment for trans men. See Mosier, "Trans Terminology"; E-Alliance, *Transgender Women Athletes and Elite Sport: A Scientific Review*, Canadian Centre for Ethics in Sport, 2022, cces.ca/transgender-women-athletes-and-elite-sport -scientific-review.

21. E-Alliance, *Transgender Women Athletes*, 2.

22. Jaime Schultz, "Good Enough? The 'Wicked' Use of Testosterone for

Defining Femaleness in Women's Sport," *Sport in Society* 24, no. 4 (2021): 607.

23. Karkazis et al., "Out of Bounds."

24. Karkazis et al., "Out of Bounds."

25. Michael A. Messner, "Sports and Male Domination: The Female Athlete as Contested Ideological Terrain," *Sociology of Sport Journal* 5, no. 3 (1988): 197–211.

26. **Gender-affirming health care** is specialized health care that meets the needs of trans and gender-diverse youth and their families, including tracking and supporting mental health, puberty blockers, and gender-affirming surgery (Mosier, "Trans Terminology").

27. Athlete Ally, "Resources," www.athleteally.org/resources.

28. Farid Saad et al., "Onset of Effects of Testosterone Treatment and Time Span Until Maximum Effects Are Achieved," *European Journal of Endocrinology* 165, no. 5 (2011): 675–85.

29. Maddie Deutsch, "Information on Testosterone Hormone Therapy," *Transgender Care*, University of California, San Francisco, 2020, transcare .ucsf.edu/article/information-testosterone-hormone-therapy.

30. International Olympic Committee, "IOC Framework on Fairness, Inclusion, and Nondiscrimination on the Basis of Gender Identity and Sex Variations," IOC, November 22, 2021, www.olympics.com/ioc/documents /athletes/ioc-framework-on-fairness-inclusion-and-non-discrimination -on-the-basis-of-gender-identity-and-sex-variations.

31. See Katie Barnes, "Premier Hockey Federation Updates Participation Policy for Transgender and Non-Binary Athletes," ESPN.com, October 15, 2021; and National Women's Soccer League, "NWSL Policy on Transgender Athletes," National Women's Soccer League, 2021.

32. Dawn Anderson-Butcher, "Youth Sport as a Vehicle for Social Development," *Kinesiology Review* 8, no. 3 (2019): 180–87; David Lubans et al., "Physical Activity for Cognitive and Mental Health in Youth: A Systematic Review of Mechanisms," *Pediatrics* 138, no. 3 (2016); Leonard M. Wankel and Bonnie G. Berger, "The Psychological and Social Benefits of Sport and Physical Activity," *Journal of Leisure Research* 22, no. 2 (1990): 167–82.

33. Project Play, *Youth Sports Facts: Participation Rates*, Aspen Institute, 2022, projectplay.org/youth-sports/facts/participation-rates.

34. Elizabeth Levy Paluck and Chelsey S. Clark, "Can Playing Together Help Us Live Together?" *Science* 369, no. 6505 (2020): 769–70.

35. David Broockman and Joshua Kalla, "Durably Reducing Transphobia: A Field Experiment on Door-to-Door Canvassing," *Science* 352, no. 6282 (2016): 220–24; Molly C. Easterlin et al., "Association of Team Sports Participation with Long-Term Mental Health Outcomes Among Individuals Exposed to Adverse Childhood Experiences," *JAMA Pediatrics* 173, no. 7 (2019): 681–88; Joshua L. Kalla and David E. Broockman, "Reducing Exclusionary Attitudes Through Interpersonal Conversation: Evidence from Three Field Experiments," *American Political Science Review* 114, no. 2 (2020): 410–25.

36. See Project Play, *Youth Sports Facts.*

37. Erin K. Howie, Bryce T. Daniels, and Justin M. Guagliano, "Promoting Physical Activity Through Youth Sports Programs: It's Social," *American Journal of Lifestyle Medicine* 14, no. 1 (2020): 78–88; Debra K. Kellstedt et al., "Youth Sport Participation and Physical Activity in Rural Communities," *Archives of Public Health*, no. 79 (2021): 1–8; Women's Sports Foundation, *Thriving Through Sport: The Transformative Impact on Girls' Mental Health*, Women's Sports Foundation, 2024.

38. ACLU of Texas, *All In for Equality Coalition Statement on Transgender Athlete Ban Bill*, ACLU of Texas, May 17, 2023, www.aclutx.org/en/press-releases/all-equality-coalition-statement-transgender-athlete-ban-bill; and Movement Advancement Project, *Bans on Transgender Youth Participation in Sports*, www.lgbtmap.org/equality-maps/youth/sports_participation_bans.

39. Movement Advancement Project, *Bans on Transgender People Using Public Bathrooms and Facilities According to Their Gender Identity*, www.lgbtmap.org/equality-maps/youth/school_bathroom_bans.

40. *Changing the Game*, directed by Michael Bartnett (2019).

41. Soule et al. v. Connecticut Association of Schools, Inc. et al., No. 3:2020cv00201 (D. Connecticut 2020).

42. Lori Riley, "Federal Judge Dismisses Lawsuit That Sought to Block

Transgender Female Athletes from Competing in Girls High School Sports in Connecticut," *Hartford Courant*, April 26, 2021, www.courant .com/2021/04/26/federal-judge-dismisses-lawsuit-that-sought-to-block -transgender-female-athletes-from-competing-in-girls-high-school -sports-in-connecticut.

43. Riley, "Federal Judge Dismisses Lawsuit."

44. Chris Mosier and Danne Lieberman, "Trans and Nonbinary Inclusion in College Sports—101," Virtual training hosted by Athlete Ally and Transathlete.com, April 19, 2023.

45. Dawn Ennis, "What Donald Trump's Transphobia Really Means for Women's Sports," *Forbes*, February 18, 2021; Paul Newberry, "Column: Trans Athletes Not an Issue but Discrimination Real," Associated Press, March 27, 2021.

46. Movement Advancement Project, *Transgender Youth Participation*.

47. Movement Advancement Project, *Transgender Youth Participation*.

48. Trans Legislation Tracker, *Tracking the Rise of Anti-Trans Bills in the U.S.*, translegislation.com/learn.

49. Michael Messner, "Gender Ideologies, Youth Sports, and the Production of Soft Essentialism," *Sociology of Sport Journal* 28, no. 2 (2011): 161.

50. Chris W. Surprenant, "Striking a Balance Between Fairness in Competition and the Rights of Transgender Athletes," *The Conversation*, May 18, 2021, theconversation.com/striking-a-balance-between-fairness -in-competition-and-the-rights-of-transgender-athletes-159685.

51. Anna Baeth and Anna Goorevich, "Mediated Moral Panics: Trans Athlete Spectres, the Haunting of Cisgender Girls and Politicians as Moral Entrepreneurs in 2021," in *Justice for Trans Athletes, Challenges and Struggles*, ed. Ali Durham Greey and Heather Jefferson Lenskyj (Emerald, 2022), 137–49.

52. Nikki Haley, "We Must Protect Women's Sports," *National Review*, February 8, 2021.

53. Baeth and Goorevich, "Mediated Moral Panics."

54. Stephanie Burnett, "Fact Check: Do Trans Athletes Have an Advantage?" *Deutsche Welle*, July 24, 2021.

55. Alyssa Jackson, "The High Cost of Being Transgender," CNN, July 31, 2015, www.cnn.com/2015/07/31/health/transgender-costs-irpt/index.html.

56. Lieve Anne Willemsen et al., "Just as Tall on Testosterone: A Neutral to Positive Effect on Adult Height of GnRHa and Testosterone in Trans Boys," *Journal of Clinical Endocrinology & Metabolism* 108, no. 2 (2023): 414–21.

57. **Drag** is a performance of exaggerated femininity, masculinity, or other forms of gender expression, usually for entertainment. Drag usually involves cross-dressing. A drag queen is someone (usually male) who performs femininely and a drag king is someone (usually female) who performs masculinely. Performances often involve comedy, social satire, and political commentary. Drag may be used as a form of protest. Drag can be used as a noun, as in the expression *in drag*, or as an adjective, as in *drag show*. According to the Movement Advancement Project, drag is "a vital part of LGBTQ culture and history. While state laws restricting gender-based dress also date back to at least the 1800s, 2023 brought a resurgence of efforts to limit free speech and expression in the form of drag. . . . These attacks are part of a much broader and coordinated effort attacking gender expression, trans people, and the LGBTQ community more broadly." **Cross-dressing** is the act of wearing clothes traditionally or stereotypically associated with a different gender. From as early as premodern history, cross-dressing has been practiced to disguise, comfort, entertain, and express oneself. Cross-dressing refers to an action or a behavior, without implying a specific motive; thus, cross-dressing is not synonymous with being trans.

3. Are Trans Athletes Dangerous?

1. "Executive Order 14201 of February 5, 2025, Keeping Men Out of Women's Sports," *Federal Register* 90, no. 27 (2025): 9279–81, www.govinfo.gov/app/details/FR-2025-02-11/2025-02513.

2. Women's Sports Policy Working Group, "Access to Female Athletes' Locker Rooms Should Be Restricted to Female Athletes," Women's Sports Policy Working Group, January 24, 2025.

3. Michael A. Messner, "When Bodies Are Weapons," *Peace Review* 4, no. 3 (1992): 28–31.

4. Lindsey Darvin, "Why Conversations About Caitlin Clark, Angel Reese and WNBA Physicality Should Be Led by Women's Sports Analysts," *Forbes*, June 5, 2024.

5. Chris Mosier and Danne Lieberman, "Trans and Nonbinary Inclusion in College Sports—101," Virtual training hosted by Athlete Ally and Transathlete.com, April 19, 2023.

6. Mosier and Lieberman, "Trans and Nonbinary Inclusion in College Sports."

7. Anna Baeth and Anna Goorevich, "Mediated Moral Panics: Trans Athlete Spectres, the Haunting of Cisgender Girls and Politicians as Moral Entrepreneurs in 2021," in *Justice for Trans Athletes, Challenges and Struggles*, ed. Ali Durham Greey and Heather Jefferson Lenskyj (Emerald, 2022), 137–49.

8. Jaime Schultz, "The Ethics of Sex Testing in Sport," in *Routledge Handbook of Sport and Exercise Systems Genetics*, ed. J. Timothy Lightfoot, Monica Hubal, and Stephen Roth (Routledge, 2019), 475–84.

9. Katrina Karkazis et al., "Out of Bounds? A Critique of the New Policies on Hyperandrogenism in Elite Female Athletes," *American Journal of Bioethics* 12, no. 7 (2012): 3–16; Katrina Karkazis and Morgan Carpenter, "Impossible 'Choices': The Inherent Harms of Regulating Women's Testosterone in Sport," *Journal of Bioethical Inquiry*, no. 15 (2018): 579–87; and Nancy Leong, "Against Women's Sports," *Washington University Law Review*, no. 95 (2017): 1249–1324.

10. Lindsay Parks Pieper, "Policing Womanhood: The International Olympic Committee, Sex Testing and the Maintenance of Hetero-Femininity in Sport" (PhD diss., Ohio State University, 2013). See also Roger Pielke Jr., "Sugar, Spice and Everything Nice: How to End 'Sex Testing' in International Athletics," *International Journal of Sport Policy and Politics* 9, no. 4 (2017): 649–65; and Schultz, "Ethics of Sex Testing."

11. Erin Buzuvis, "Hormone Check: Critique of Olympic Rules on Sex and Gender," *Wisconsin Journal of Law, Gender & Society*, no. 31 (2016): 29–55. Benjamin James Ingram and Connie Lynn Thomas, "Transgender

Policy in Sport: A Review of Current Policy and Commentary of the Challenges of Policy Creation," *Current Sports Medicine Reports* 18, no. 6 (2019): 239–47.

12. Pieper, "Policing Womanhood."

13. Ingram and Thomas, "Transgender Policy in Sport," 240.

14. Planned Parenthood, "What's Intersex?," Planned Parenthood, www.plannedparenthood.org/learn/gender-identity/sex-gender-identity/whats-intersex.

15. Anne Fausto-Sterling, "The Five Sexes: Why Male and Female Are Not Enough," *The Sciences* 33, no. 2 (1993): 20–24.

16. Marion Müller, "Constructing Gender Incommensurability in Competitive Sport: Sex/Gender Testing and the New Regulations on Female Hyperandrogenism," *Human Studies*, no. 39 (2016): 405–31.

17. Mosier and Lieberman, "Trans and Nonbinary Inclusion in College Sports."

18. Erin Buzuvis, "Caster Semenya and the Myth of a Level Playing Field," *Modern American*, no. 6 (2010): 36–42; Cheryl Cooky and Shari L. Dworkin, "Policing the Boundaries of Sex: A Critical Examination of Gender Verification and the Caster Semenya Controversy," *Journal of Sex Research* 50, no. 2 (2013): 103–11; and Jamie Schultz, "Caster Semenya and the 'Question of Too': Sex Testing in Elite Women's Sport and the Issue of Advantage," *Quest* 63, no. 2 (2011): 228–43.

19. Estadão, "Pedro Spajari melhora desempenho após descobrir doença rara," *Estadão*, August 24, 2018, www.estadao.com.br/esportes/pedro-spajari-melhora-desempenho-apos-descobrir-doenca-rara.

20. To learn more about the history and impact of these regulations, we recommend the documentary *Category: Woman*, directed by Phyllis Ellis, 2022.

21. Carlos Maza and Luke Brinker, "15 Experts Debunk Right-Wing Transgender Bathroom Myth," *Media Matters for America*, March 20, 2014.

22. Brian S. Barnett, Ariana E. Nesbit, and Renée M. Sorrentino, "The Transgender Bathroom Debate at the Intersection of Politics, Law, Ethics,

and Science," *Journal of the American Academy of Psychiatry and the Law* 46, no. 2 (2018): 233.

23. Jody L. Herman, "Gendered Restrooms and Minority Stress: The Public Regulation of Gender and Its Impact on Transgender People's Lives," *Journal of Public Management & Social Policy* 19, no. 1 (2013): 65–80.

24. Sandy James et al., *The Report of the 2015 US Transgender Survey* (Washington, DC: National Center for Transgender Equality, 2016), 224–30.

25. Gabriel R. Murchison et al., "School Restroom and Locker Room Restrictions and Sexual Assault Risk Among Transgender Youth," *Pediatrics* 143, no. 6 (2019): e20182902.

26. Katelyn Burns, "Women Are Getting Harassed in Bathrooms Because of Anti-Transgender Hysteria," *Vox*, May 5, 2016.

27. Lara Stemple, Andrew Flores, and Ilan H. Meyer, "Sexual Victimization Perpetrated by Women: Federal Data Reveal Surprising Prevalence," *Aggression and Violent Behavior*, no. 34 (2017): 302–11.

28. Michael J. Fliotsos et al., "Prevalence, Patterns, and Characteristics of Eye Injuries in Professional Mixed Martial Arts," *Clinical Ophthalmology* (2021): 2759–66.

29. Dennis Romboy, "Why Sen. Mike Lee Opposes Transgender Women Competing in Women's Sports," *Deseret News*, December 29, 2020.

30. Trevor Project, "The Trevor Project Research Brief: LGBTQ and Gender-Affirming Spaces," *Trevor Project*, December 2020.

31. Trevor Project, "2023 U.S. National Survey on the Mental Health of LGBTQ Young People," *E-Journal Menara Perkebunan* 82, no. 1 (2023).

32. Trevor Project, "Research Brief."

33. K.C. Councilor, "The Specter of Trans Bodies: Public and Political Discourse About 'Bathroom Bills,'" in *The Routledge Handbook of Gender and Communication*, ed. Marnel Niles Goins, Joan Faber McAlister, and Bryant Keith Alexander (Routledge, 2020), 274–88.

34. Amira Hasenbush, Andrew R. Flores, and Jody L. Herman, "Gender Identity Nondiscrimination Laws in Public Accommodations: A

Review of Evidence Regarding Safety and Privacy in Public Restrooms, Locker Rooms, and Changing Rooms," *Sexuality Research and Social Policy* 16, no. 1 (2019): 70–83.

35. Tynslei Spence-Mitchell, "Restroom Restrictions: How Race and Sexuality Have Affected Bathroom Legislation," *Gender, Work & Organization* 28 (2021): 14–20.

36. Baeth and Goorevich, "Mediated Moral Panics."

37. Jaime Schultz et al., "The Future of Women's Sport Includes Transgender Women and Girls," in *Justice for Trans Athletes*, ed. Ali Durham Greey and Helen Lenskyj (Emerald, 2022), 17–29.

38. David Crary and Lindsay Whitehurst, "Lawmakers Can't Cite Local Examples of Trans Girls in Sports," Associated Press, March 3, 2021.

39. Baeth and Goorevich, "Mediated Moral Panics."

40. Nancy Neuman, "Opinion: In Trans Debate, Stand Up for Girls," *Altoona Mirror*, May 29, 2021.

41. Baeth and Goorevich, "Mediated Moral Panics."

42. R. Shep Melnick, "The Transformation of Title IX: Regulating Gender Equality in Education," Brookings Institution Press, 2018.

43. Ellen J. Staurowsky et al., "Chasing Equity: The Triumphs, Challenges, and Opportunities in Sports for Girls and Women," Women's Sports Foundation, 2020.

44. Schultz et al., "Future of Women's Sport."

45. Russel Contreras, "The Forces Behind Anti-Trans Bills Across the U.S.," *Axios*, March 31, 2023.

46. Staurowsky et al., "Chasing Equity."

47. Project Play, *Youth Sports Facts: Participation Rates*, Aspen Institute, 2022, projectplay.org/youth-sports/facts/participation-rates.

48. Jennifer Turnnidge, Jean Côté, and David J. Hancock, "Positive Youth Development From Sport to Life: Explicit or Implicit Transfer?," *Quest* 66, no. 2 (2014): 203–17.

49. Andrew J. Martin, "Examining a Multidimensional Model of Student Motivation and Engagement Using a Construct Validation

Approach," *British Journal of Educational Psychology* 77, no. 2 (2007): 413–40.

50. Elizabeth Levy Paluck and Chelsey S. Clark, "Can Playing Together Help Us Live Together?," *Science* 369, no. 6505 (2020): 769–70.

51. Joshua L. Kalla and David E. Broockman, "Reducing Exclusionary Attitudes Through Interpersonal Conversation: Evidence from Three Field Experiments," *American Political Science Review* 114, no. 2 (2020): 410–25.

52. Marc Ramirez, "Homophobic Speech in Youth Sports Doesn't Just Harm Gay Boys. It Harms Straight Boys Too," *USA TODAY*, September 13, 2024.

53. Laura J. Wernick et al., "Policing Gender and Sexuality in High School Sports: The Mediating Impact of Hearing Anti-LGBTQ+ Language on High School Athletes' Self-Esteem Across Gender Identity, Sexual Orientation, and Race," *Journal of Sport and Social Issues* 47, no. 6 (2023): 504–34.

54. Wernick et al., "Policing Gender."

55. **Gender-affirming surgery** is a procedure that alters one's appearance and/or changes one's sexual characteristics to align with one's gender identity. For example, a trans man may undergo a masculinization surgery like top surgery to reconstruct his chest, while a trans woman may undergo a surgery for facial feminization and/or breast augmentation. Cis people also undergo gender-affirming surgery, but we do not frame it that way. Breast implants or reductions, laser hair removal, cool sculpting, Botox, nose jobs, hair implants, lip filler, and brow lifts are all gender-affirming procedures that cis folks access regularly without restriction. Intersex babies often undergo similar procedures. Because it is without their consent, it is not considered gender-affirming surgery. See Chris Mosier, "Trans Terminology," Transathlete, www.transathlete.com/starthere.

56. **Tucking** is a technique sometimes used by trans women to feel better about their gender presentation. Methods include using gaffer tape, gaff underwear, and compression underwear to smooth and flatten the groin area. **Binding** is a technique sometimes used by trans men to feel better about their gender presentation. Methods include using tight clothing, tape, and compression garments to smooth and flatten the chest area.

4. How Do We Better Support All Girls' and Women's Sports?

1. Heather McGhee, *The Sum of Us: What Racism Costs Everyone and How We Can Prosper Together* (One World, 2022).

2. McGhee, *Sum of Us*, 14.

3. McGhee, *Sum of Us*, 8.

4. Ellen J. Staurowsky et al., "Chasing Equity: The Triumphs, Challenges, and Opportunities in Sports for Girls and Women," Women's Sports Foundation, 2020.

5. Sheila Mitchell, "Women's Participation in the Olympic Games 1900–1926," *Journal of Sport History* 4, no. 2 (1977): 208–28.

6. Olympic Games, "Olympic Games Athens 1896 Results," International Olympic Committee, 2024, olympics.com/en/olympic-games/athens-1896/results.

7. Danielle L. Cormier et al., "Grit in Sport: A Scoping Review," *International Review of Sport and Exercise Psychology* 17, no. 1 (2024): 1–38.

8. Patricia Vertinsky, "Exercise, Physical Capability, and the Eternally Wounded Woman in Late Nineteenth Century North America," *Journal of Sport History* 14, no. 1 (1987): 7–27.

9. Ellen J. Stauroswky et al., "50 Years of Title IX: We're Not Done Yet," Women's Sports Foundation May 4, 2022, www.womenssportsfoundation.org/articles_and_report/50-years-of-title-ix-were-not-done-yet.

10. Stephen Lane, *Long Run to Glory: The Story of the Greatest Marathon in Olympic History and the Women Who Made it Happen* (Rowman & Littlefield, 2023).

11. Jaime Schultz, *Qualifying Times: Points of Change in US Women's Sport* (University of Illinois Press, 2014).

12. RecLeaguer, 2025, www.recleaguer.com.

13. Jaime Schultz et al., "The Future of Women's Sport Includes Transgender Women and Girls," in *Justice for Trans Athletes*, ed. Ali Durham Greey and Helen Lenskyj (Emerald, 2022), 17–29.

14. Schultz et al., "Future of Women's Sport.

15. Schultz et al., "Future of Women's Sport.

16. Shoshana K. Goldberg, "Fair Play: The Importance of Sports Participation for Transgender Youth," Center for American Progress, February 8, 2021, www.americanprogress.org/article/fair-play.

17. David Crary and Lindsay Whitehurst, "Lawmakers Can't Cite Local Examples of Trans Girls in Sports," Associated Press, March 3, 2021.

18. Vikki Krane, Emma Calow, and Brandy Panunti, "Female Testosterone: Contested Terrain," *Kinesiology Review* 11, no. 1 (2021): 54–63.

19. Krane, Calow, and Panunti, "Female Testosterone."

20. Elizabeth A. Sharrow, "Sports, Transgender Rights and the Bodily Politics of Cisgender Supremacy," *Laws* 10, no. 3 (2021): 63.

21. Sharrow, "Sports, Transgender Rights."

22. Human Rights Watch, "They're Chasing Us Away from Sport," Human Rights Watch, December 4, 2020.

23. Sharrow, "Sports, Transgender Rights."

24. One's **gender expression** is the way a person communicates their gender to others through external means such as clothing, hairstyles, appearance, and/or mannerisms. One's gender expression does not necessarily indicate what a person's pronouns may be or what their gender identity may be (Mosier, "Trans Terminology"). Sport, particularly women's sport, is a place where all people and people designated female at birth can express themselves outside of the stereotypes of what a "woman" should be. We've seen leagues, teams, and players embrace style and expression in the pregame fit checks and in on-court expression as well. In our interviews, several of the athletes talked about sport being a place they could get away with their gender expression of choice. Baggy shorts, for example, can provide trans athletes cover and allow for a more authentic gender expression with less harassment. (See Chris Mosier, "Trans Terminology," www.transathlete.com/starthere.)

25. Schultz et al., "Future of Women's Sport."

26. Schultz et al., "Future of Women's Sport."

27. Women's Sports Foundation, "Billie Jean King, Megan Rapinoe, and Candace Parker Join Nearly 200 Athletes Supporting Trans Youth Par-

ticipation in Sports," Women's Sports Foundation, December 21, 2020, www.womenssportsfoundation.org/press_release/billie-jean-king-megan -rapinoe-and-candace-parker-join-nearly-200-athletes-supporting-trans -youth-participation-in-sports.

28. Sex is assigned at birth, and names are given at birth too. Many trans folks will change their name from the name assigned to them at birth to a name that is more aligned with their sex, gender, and/or social identity. The name assigned to them at birth can be referred to as their **dead-name** (see Mosier, "Trans Terminology"). Respecting name and pronoun changes is important because people will use deadnames and pronouns assigned at birth intentionally to deny who the trans person is. Many cis people choose to change their name when they get married. How easily society makes this shift points to our ability to shift as language and identity shift.

29. Joseph G. Kosciw et al., *The 2019 National School Climate Survey: The Experiences of Lesbian, Gay, Bisexual, Transgender, and Queer Youth in Our Nation's Schools. A Report from GLSEN* (Gay, Lesbian and Straight Education Network [GLSEN], 2020).

30. Movement Advancement Project, "Equality Maps: Bans on Transgender Youth Participation in Sports, Movement Advancement Project," 2024, www.mapresearch.org/equality-maps/youth /sports_participation_bans.

31. Movement Advancement Project, "Equality Maps."

32. Chris Mosier, "Resources: Links," Transathlete, 2024, www .transathlete.com/links.

33. Mosier, "Resources: Links."

34. Mosier, "Resources: Links."

35. Eileen McDonagh and Laura Pappano, *Playing with the Boys: Why Separate Is Not Equal in Sports* (Oxford University Press, 2007).

36. Emma S. Cowley et al., "'Invisible Sportswomen': The Sex Data Gap in Sport and Exercise Science Research," *Women in Sport and Physical Activity Journal* 29, no. 2 (2021): 146–51.

37. See Rebekka J. Findlay et al., "How the Menstrual Cycle and Menstruation Affect Sporting Performance: Experiences and Perceptions of

Elite Female Rugby Players," *British Journal of Sports Medicine* 54, no. 18 (2020): 1108–13; Trent A. Petrie and Christy A. Greenleaf, "Eating Disorders in Sport: From Theory to Research to Intervention," *Handbook of Sport Psychology* (2007): 352–78; Jaime Schultz, "Discipline and Push-Up: Female Bodies, Femininity, and Sexuality in Popular Representations of Sports Bras," *Sociology of Sport Journal* 21, no. 2 (2004): 185–205.

38. Julie Brice, Holly Thorpe, Belinda Wheaton, and Robyn Longhurst, "Postfeminism, Consumption and Activewear: Examining Women Consumers' Relationship with the Postfeminine Ideal," *Journal of Consumer Culture* 23, no. 3 (2023): 617–36; Maria Fenech, "A Study of Challenges That Transgender Athletes Face in Sports," in *Mapping the Rainbow* vol. 3 (Human Rights Directorate 2024), 143.

39. Stauroswky et al., "50 Years of Title IX."

40. Stauroswky et al., "50 Years of Title IX."

41. Tara D. Shonenshine, "Women and Sports: 50 Years After Title IX, Is the Playing Field Level?" *The Hill*, June 20, 2022.

42. See Hannah Grabenstein, "Are the 2024 Paris Olympics Gender Equal? That Depends How You Measure It," *PBS NewsHour*, August 2, 2024.

43. Ellen J. Staurowsky et al., "Chasing Equity: The Triumphs, Challenges, and Opportunities in Sports for Girls and Women," Women's Sports Foundation, January 15, 2020.

44. U.S. Department of Education, *Equity in Athletics Disclosure Act Data: Analysis Cutting Tool*, U.S. Department of Education, ope.ed.gov /athletics.

45. Staurowsky et al., "Chasing Equity."

46. Staurowsky et al., "Chasing Equity."

47. Laura J. Burton and Sarah Leberman, eds., *Women in Sport Leadership: Research and Practice for Change* (Taylor & Francis, 2017).

48. Burton and Leberman, *Women in Sport.*

49. Elizabeth A. Joy et al., "Sexual Violence in Sport: Expanding Awareness and Knowledge for Sports Medicine Providers," *Current Sports Medicine Reports* 20, no. 10 (2021): 531–39.

50. M. B. Nolan, "The Unstoppable Ambition of Women in Sports,"

Shondaland, September 18, 2023, sports.yahoo.com/wnba-salaries -highest-league-average-140000974.html.

51. Schultz et al., "Future of Women's Sport."

52. Cheryl Cooky et al., "One and Done: The Long Eclipse of Women's Televised Sports, 1989–2019," *Communication & Sport* 9, no. 3 (2021): 347–71.

53. Anna Baeth et al., "Representation Matter(ing)s: Visibility Politics and Mediated Coverage of LGBTQI+ Athletes in 2021," *Communication in Sport* (forthcoming).

54. Anna Baeth and Anna Goorevich, "Mediated Moral Panics: Trans Athlete Spectres, the Haunting of Cisgender Girls and Politicians as Moral Entrepreneurs in 2021," in *Justice for Trans Athletes, Challenges and Struggles*, ed. Ali Durham Greey and Heather Jefferson Lenskyj (Emerald, 2022), 137–49.

55. Stauroswky et al., "50 Years of Title IX."

56. See Athlete Ally, "Resources," Athlete Ally, www.athleteally.org /resources; and Mosier, "Resources: Links."

57. Anna Baeth and A. Kurtz, "Athlete Ally Athletic Equality Index: Addendum—Religiously Affiliated Institutions," Athlete Ally Athletic Equality Index, aei.athleteally.org/wp-content/uploads/2021/04/AEI -Addendum_-Religiously-Affiliated-Institutions.pdf.

58. Baeth and Kurtz, "Athlete Ally Athletic Equality Index."

59. Baeth and Kurtz, "Athlete Ally Athletic Equality Index."

60. Nancy Hogshead-Makar, "Sex Matters: Why Transgender Athletes Must Not Compete Against Biological Females," *Swimming World*, January 25, 2024.

61. Hogshead-Makar, "Sex Matters."

62. Hogshead-Makar, "Sex Matters."

63. Associated Press, "College Swimmers, Volleyball Players Sue NCAA Over Transgender Policies," Associated Press, March 14, 2024.

64. Gaines v. National Collegiate Athletic Association, 1:24-cv-01109 (N.D. Ga.); "ACLU: Gaines v. NCAA," *American Civil Liberties Union*, September 30, 2024, www.aclu.org/cases/gaines-v-ncaa.

65. Erin Nichols, Adele Pavlidis, and Raphaël Nowak, "'It's Like Lifting the Power': Powerlifting, Digital Gendered Subjectivities, and the Politics of Multiplicity," *Leisure Sciences* 46, no. 3 (2024): 254–73.

66. Twin Cities Goodtime Sports League, "Twin Cities Goodtime Sports League History," Twin Cities Goodtime Sports League, tcgsl .sportngin.com/page/show/6900743-history.

67. Twin Cities Goodtime Sports League, "History."

68. Katie Barnes, "The 'Magic' and Faith Within the WNBA's Most Powerful Player," ESPN.com, June 24, 2021.

69. José Esteban Muñoz, *Cruising Utopia: The Then and There of Queer Futurity* (New York University Press, 2009).

70. Muñoz, *Cruising Utopia*, 96.

71. Muñoz, *Cruising Utopia*, 189.

Conclusion

1. Elizabeth Levy Paluck and Chelsey S. Clark, "Can Playing Together Help Us Live Together?," *Science* 369, no. 6505 (August 2020): 769–70.

2. David E. Broockman and Joshua Kalla, "Durably Reducing Transphobia: A Field Experiment on Door-to-Door Canvassing," *Science* 352, no. 6282 (2016): 220–24; Molly C. Easterlin et al., "Association of Team Sports Participation with Long-Term Mental Health Outcomes Among Individuals Exposed to Adverse Childhood Experiences," *JAMA Pediatrics* 173, no. 7 (2019): 681–88; Joshua L. Kalla and David E. Broockman, "Reducing Exclusionary Attitudes Through Interpersonal Conversation: Evidence from Three Field Experiments," *American Political Science Review* 114, no. 2 (2020): 410–25.

3. Judith Butler, *Undoing Gender* (Routledge, 2004), 29.

Authors' Note

1. **Nibling** is a gender-neutral term used instead of niece or nephew.

2. Audre Lorde, "The Uses of the Erotic," in *Sister Outsider: Essays and Speeches* (Crossing, 1984).

3. Anti-Oppression Network, "Allyship," Anti-Oppression Network, December 15, 2023, theantioppressionnetwork.com/allyship.

4. Anti-Oppression Network, "Allyship."

5. Anna Baeth, "Becoming Allied: A Capacious and Reflexive Account of LGBTQI+ Research, Quakerism, and Sport," in *Social Justice Through Sport and Exercise Psychology*, ed. Leslee A. Fisher (Routledge, 2025), 246–59.

6. Elizabeth Grosz, *Volatile Bodies: Toward a Corporeal Feminism* (St. Leonards, NSW: Indiana University Press, 1994).

Appendix A: Suggested Pathways to Play

1. **Puberty blockers** pause the onset of puberty in a young person, which affords them time to make decisions about their care. Puberty blockers are used regularly for cis youths with precocious puberty, but the same medications are banned for trans youths in twenty-five states. (See Chris Mosier, "Trans Terminology," www.transathlete.com/starthere.)

2. Some trans and gender-nonconforming folks decide to undergo **gender-affirming hormone treatment** (GAHT), previously and commonly referred to as **hormone replacement therapy** (HRT), which includes taking certain sex hormone suppressants and administering other sex hormones so that secondary sexual characteristics more closely align with one's gender identity. For example, a trans man may choose to take testosterone, which may lead to more muscle tone, a deeper voice, and facial hair. A trans woman may choose to suppress testosterone and start estrogen treatment, which may lead to changes like softer skin, less muscle mass, more body fat, and breast development.

INDEX

ABOUT THE AUTHORS

Ellie Roscher (she/they) is a writer, educator, podcaster, coach, and speaker. She was a two-sport college athlete, is the author of several books, and lives in Minneapolis.

Dr. Anna Baeth (she/her) is a critical feminist scholar and a cultural studies practitioner of sport. She is the vice president of programs and research at Athlete Ally.

PUBLISHING IN THE PUBLIC INTEREST

Thank you for reading this book published by The New Press; we hope you enjoyed it. New Press books and authors play a crucial role in sparking conversations about the key political and social issues of our day.

We hope that you will stay in touch with us. To keep up to date with our books, events, and the issues we cover, follow us on social media and sign up for our newsletter at thenewpress.org.

Please consider buying New Press books not only for yourself, but also for friends and family and to donate to schools, libraries, community centers, prison libraries, and other organizations involved with the issues our authors write about.

The New Press is a 501(c)(3) nonprofit organization; if you wish to support our work with a tax-deductible gift please visit https://thenewpress.org/donate/ or use the QR code below.